KT-571-699

For Remy - Alan

For Tanya, a huge animal lover - Sarah

With thanks to zoologist Megan Roe for her tireless fact checking and to editor Helen Carr and all at The O'Brien Press; always a pleasure to work with.

ANIMAL CRACKERS

Brought to you by the crack ANIMAL CRACKERS team of ALAN and SARAH...

LET'S GO ANIMAL CRACKERS!

LOVE ANIMALS? LOVE LAUGHING? JUMP STRAIGHT IN!

(...and their good friend, HOPPY!)

HI! I'M HOPPY!

First published 2020 by
The O'Brien Press Ltd,
12 Terenure Road East, Rathgar,
Dublin 6, D06 HD27, Ireland.

Tel: +353 1 4923333;
Fax: +353 1 4922777

Email: books@obrien.ie

Website: www.obrien.ie

The O'Brien Press is a member of Publishing Ireland.

ISBN: 978-1-78849-065-8

Image credits: p46 (frame on horse), pp 86-87 (map), p136 (3D globe), 168 (human shape)
Shutterstock; used with permission.

7 6 5 4 3 2 1
24 23 22 21 20

Printed and bound in Drukarnia Skleniarz, Poland.
The paper in this book is produced using pulp from managed forests.

Printed in

ANIMAL CRACKERS

FANTASTIC FACTS ABOUT YOUR FAVOURITE ANIMALS

SARAH WEBB & ALAN NOLAN

THE O'BRIEN PRESS
DUBLIN

CONTENTS

PART 4
Animals All Around Ireland

PART 5
Where in the World? Animal Habitats

PART 6
Please Take Care of Us

Introduction

This is Alan.

This is Sarah.

Together they are 'Animal Crackers'

Oi!

Careful with that tusk!

Alan is dotty about dogs.

Sarah is nutty for narwhals (and bottlenose dolphins, and blue whales and humpback whales).

Join them on an epic animal journey
as they travel deep into deepest oceans,
far into the jungle-iest jungles and
even under your own doormat
in search of some of the wildest and
most wonderful creatures on the planet.

They have invited their good friend,
Hoppy to guide you through their favourite
facts about the animal kingdom.

Hi, I'm Hoppy the tree frog and I'll be hopping through the book by your side. I won't hold your hand though as mine are rather sticky! Helps me hang upside down on the jungle trees, you see.

Are you ready?
Jump straight in with me!

Let's go Animal Crackers!

So, what's your favourite animal?

Are you cat crazy?

MY FAVOURITE

TIGER

MY FAVOURITE

CHEETAH

MY FAVOURITE

KITTEN

Are you a hamster, mouse or a gerbil lover?

MY FAVOURITE

MOUSE

MY FAVOURITE

GERBIL

What about me?

Or me?

Or me?

Are you monkey mad?

MY FAVOURITE

CHIMPANZEE

MY FAVOURITE

GORILLA

MY FAVOURITE

YOUR BABY BROTHER

Are you a frog super fan?

And honestly, who wouldn't be?
We are both fascinating and adorable!

Pick me!

MY FAVOURITE

Or are you dotty about dogs like Alan?

Then read on!

PART 1

Some of Our Favourite Animals

The Wonderful World of Dogs

Let's start our animal journey with Alan's favourite animal (and maybe yours too), dogs.

And the top pet choice is . . . you got it, a DOG!

Did you know that over 46% of families in Ireland have a pet?

HEY! What about me?

Don't worry, cats are number two, followed by fish.

Fish, yum.

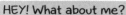

Fluffy! Fluffy, can we please have Tiddler back? We need him later.

And watch out for his teeth!

You know that fish is a red-bellied piranha, right?!

P-TOO!

Heh, heh.

The favourite dog breed in Ireland is the Labrador. Lots of people think Labradors are from Labrador in Canada, but they are actually from Newfoundland, a large island off Canada.

I'm more interested in a tan than swimming.

They used to be known as St John's Water Dogs or Lesser Newfoundlands. It was actually an English man who renamed them Labradors in the 1830s. He brought some home from Newfoundland, called him his 'Labrador dogs' and the name stuck!

Hoppy's Paws for Thought

Dogs have up to 300 million smell receptors in their noses. Humans only have around 6 million. Dogs can smell things that are up to 12 metres underground. They are master sniffers! This is why dogs are used for tracking people who are lost or buried in rubble after earthquakes.

Hot Dog!

Dogs sweat through their feet – so if you're shaking paws with a dog make sure to wash your hands afterwards!

All dogs are direct descendants of wolves. Want to know more about how dogs became tame? Follow me!

A Very Short History of Dogs

Dogs were the first species (or kind) of animals to be tamed and to live with humans.

But how and when did this happen?

Between 20 and 40 thousand years ago (no one is sure of the exact date) grey wolves started to interact with early humans. They travelled with the humans and ate their leftover scraps. They barked to warn the humans that predators were around. They also helped them hunt.

There are pictures of dogs in cave drawings and cave carvings that are thousands of years old.

Over the years these wolves became less and less fierce.

Ancient Egyptians used dogs for hunting and guarding.

There are now over 300 different breeds of dog.

It is one of the most diverse species in the world.

Hoppy's Fun Facts

The Ancient Chinese bred dogs to look like little lions. These were called Pekingese. They were named after the capital city, Peking, now called Beijing. Chinese Emperors used to carry these small dogs in the sleeves of their robes!

How to Draw a Dog

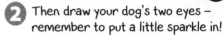

It's so easy!

1 First, draw the ears and hair on the top of your dog's head

2 Then draw your dog's two eyes – remember to put a little sparkle in!

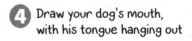

3 Draw your dog's oval-shaped nose and colour it black

4 Draw your dog's mouth, with his tongue hanging out

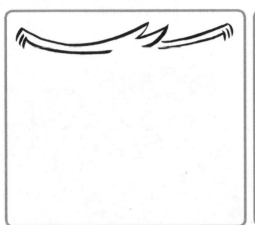

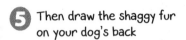

5 Then draw the shaggy fur on your dog's back

6 Draw your dog's front legs and his furry tummy

7 Then give your dog a waggly tail

8 Finally, draw your dog's back legs and give him some fur texture – WOOF!

Ah! C'est magnifique!

Wild about Wolves

All dogs are descended from wolves, the biggest kind of wild dogs.

Other wild dogs include dingoes (who live in Australia) and foxes. We have lots of red foxes in Ireland. You may have even seen one in your garden!

Fairy tales are full of scary wolves, from the wolf dressed up as grandmother in 'Little Red Riding Hood' to the baddie in 'The Three Little Pigs and the Big Bad Wolf'.

But are they really as crafty and bloodthirsty as they are made out to be?

Let's see!

There are lots of different species of wolves, but the best known is the grey wolf. It's also the largest. Grey wolves live mainly in North America, Northern Europe and Asia in forests and mountains.

Wolves gather in packs; they live and hunt together. The leaders of the pack are called the alpha female and the alpha male. They're like the mum and dad of the wolf pack and they stay together for life.

Hoppy's Paws for Thought

The fancy scientific name for animals that stay together for life and look after hunting and child rearing together is 'socially monogamous'.

3 to 5 per cent of mammals stay with their partners for life.

Socially monogamous animals include:

 Swans   Gibbon Apes

 Termites   Penguins

 Turtle Doves   Golden Eagles

 and of course, our old friends, the wolves!

Wonderful Wolves

Each wolf has its own place in the pack, they are more or less important depending on their hunting skills and on how assertive or submissive they are. Young pups compete to be king of the hill by fighting. When they grow up, the younger wolves leave to start a new pack or find a new place to live – like teenagers leaving home for the first time for college or a job!

Wolves communicate by using body language or facial expressions. If they are angry they will bare their teeth. Their tail will go up and their ears will lower.

If dogs want to play, they sometimes drop their bodies, stretch their front legs out and wag their tails. This is called the 'play bow'.

Wolves do this too! Young wolves love to play. They chase each other and have play fights.

Hoppy's Paws for Thought

Wolves, like all dogs, have an amazing sense of smell. They can smell an animal from over 2km away. And a wolf's own smell is as distinctive as a human fingerprint.

FINGERPRINT SHEET

NAME: FLUFFY

LEFT FRONT

RIGHT REAR

RIGHT FRONT

Hoppy's Paws for Thought

Wolves have brilliant hearing and sight, which makes them powerful hunters. Their jaws are extremely strong and they have forty-two big, sharp teeth, including four long canines. They can eat up to eight kilograms of food in a single meal. This would be like eating a large dog or two pet cats or thirteen pairs of shoes!

Howl Like a Wolf

Wolf calls or howls can travel over 10km in the air. Imagine being able to shout that loudly!

They howl to keep the pack together and strangers away, or to mourn or show sadness for a wolf who has died.

Why don't you try howling like a wolf?

Can You Tell Your Dalmatians from your Dachshunds?

Which dog is which? Guess the dog breed from their silhouette!

A clue for you - there is a Great Dane, a Doberman, a Poodle, a Chihuahua, a Boxer dog, a Dachshund and, of course, a Dalmation!

1

2

3

4

ANSWERS: 1. POODLE, 2. BOXER, 3. DOBERMAN, 4. CHIHUAHUA, 5. DALMATION, 6. GREAT DANE, 7. DACHSHUND

Hoppy's Paws for Thought

 Some dogs can understand around 250 words and gestures.

 Basenji dogs can't bark, but they can yodel!

 The Norwegian Lundehund has six toes on each paw.
That's a lot of toes! Most dogs have four toes on each paw.

Do All Dogs Go Woof?

What Do Dogs Say in Different Countries?

In Ireland dogs go 'woof woof'! But what noise do they make in other languages? Let's find out!

BLAF BLAF! (Afrikaans)

VOFF VOFF! (Icelandic)

BUP BUP! (Catalan)

JAFF JAFF! (Bulgarian)

WANG WANG!
(Mandarin)

WOW WOW!
(Cantonese)

WAF WAF!
(Dutch)

BOW BOW!
(Hindi)

HAU HAU!
(Polish)

AMH AMH!
(Irish)

The Incredible World of Cats

The History of Cats

Cats have been around for millions of years, but have only been domesticated in the last 5 to 10 thousand years.

The most famous early cats are the sabre-toothed cats, like the Smilodon fatalis which, lived in America. They became extinct about 12,000 years ago. They had long canine teeth and used them like daggers to stab their prey.

During the Ice Age there was an eruption of sticky black tar from under the earth near modern-day Los Angeles.
It trapped thousands of animals including 2,000 Smilodons. Their skeletons were discovered by scientists around 1901. There is now a museum at the La Brea Tar Pits where you can see over a million Ice Age fossils, including Smilodon teeth and bones.

Domestic cats, or pet cats, don't look all that different to wild cats, although wild cats are often much bigger! All cats – wild and domestic – belong to the same family of animals, the Felidae.

All cats are carnivores or flesh eaters and most hunt alone. Domestic cats are descended from the small wild cat, Felis Silvestris, which still lives in Europe, western Asia and Africa today.

Wildcats or 'Small Cats'

Wildcats, also known as 'small cats' (as opposed to 'big cats' like tigers) live mainly in forests, or on mountains. The bobcat is the most common wildcat in North America. The puma or cougar lives in North and South America and is a wildcat even though it's actually pretty big! The lynx is a wildcat that lives in Europe, North America and Asia.

There are no wildcats in Ireland anymore, but they do still live in Scotland!

Scottish wildcats live in the forests in Scotland, but they are in danger of extinction. They have stocky bodies and a short tail, and their kittens are fierce and almost impossible to tame.

Hoppy's Feline Facts

🐾 Cats have excellent eyesight, even in dim light. Their whiskers (or 'vibrissae') are also quite special. They are highly sensitive and can tell the shape and texture of any object when they brush against it. Cats can even detect change in air currents using their whiskers – letting them know when a predator may be near!

🐾 The smallest domestic cat is the Singapura. They are so small they can fit in a teacup.

🐾 The largest domestic cat is the mighty ragdoll. They are twice the size of an average pet cat!

🐾 Cats spend around two-thirds of every day asleep.

Big Cats

Most of the best known 'big cats', like the lion, the tiger, the leopard and the jaguar live in grasslands. Big cats are known for their speed and power.

Tigers

The largest and heaviest big cat is the tiger. Tigers can grow up to 2.8 metres long and can weigh up to 300kg – that's the weight of five people! They eat mostly deer and wild pigs, but also have been known to attack baby elephants.

Although most cats don't like water, tigers love to swim. The tigers who live in forests in Asia swim in the rivers to keep cool.

The Bengal tiger is the national animal of India and Bangladesh. They are endangered and could be extinct within the next ten years.

Tigers have distinctive thick black stripes on their orange bodies.

Lions

Lions are known as the 'King of the Beasts'. Ten thousand years ago they roamed Europe, Asia and America; now they are found mainly in Africa. The live together in groups called 'prides'.

Find out more about lions on page 146.

Feline Fact

Generally big cats roar and small cats purr. Scientists are studying cats' noises to this day.

Leopards

Leopards often pull their prey into a tree and eat it up there, away from jackals and other annoying wild dogs!

Amur leopards are very rare. There are only about seventy left in the world; around 60 per cent of them live in a special national park in Russia called Land of the Leopard. Snow leopards are also very rare; they live in the mountains of central Asia.

Leopards have blotchy spots on their coats that look almost like rosettes or flowers.

Jaguars

Jaguars are good swimmers and have been known to kill and eat crocodiles. They live in the tropical rain forests of Central and South America. Unfortunately, they are in danger of extinction as the forests where they live are being cut down.

Jaguars have interesting markings – black dots inside splodges on their golden coats. Sadly, their coats are so beautiful that they are hunted for their fur.

Cheetahs

The fastest land animal on earth is the cheetah. Cheetahs can run three times as fast as humans. After catching and killing its prey, a cheetah is so tired it needs to rest for half an hour before it has the energy to eat.

Although they are large in size, cheetahs are not technically Big Cats as they purr instead of roar. Cheetahs have black spots on their golden coats.

A Coat of Many Colours

Can You Guess the Big Cat Coat?

5

6

ANSWERS: 1. TIGER, 2. LEOPARD, 3. CHEETAH,
4. JAGUAR, 5. LION, 6. PANTHER

Hoppy's Feline Facts

Irish monks drew tiny pictures of cats into the Book of Kells. There is also a famous poem written by a monk about his cat. It's called 'Pangur Bán'. The monk says 'Hunting mice is his delight, hunting words I sit all night.'

Domestic Cats and Pet Cats

Do you have a pet cat? There are over 500 million domesticated cats in the world today – that's a lot of pet cats!

Cats first started living with humans between 5,000 and 10,000 years ago. They were very useful – they caught rats and mice in the grain stores and in homes.

Pet cats still show off their hunting skills – by catching rodents and birds.

NAUGHTY FLUFFY! LET GO OF POLLY!

Cats were sacred to the Ancient Egyptians. When someone died, their cats were often wrapped in bandages and made into cat mummies. They were put in a special mummy casing and placed in the tomb with their master or mistress.

The Ancient Egyptian work for cat was 'Mau'. If you killed a cat in Ancient Egypt you could be put to death – yikes!

Cat Superstitions

In medieval times people thought that witches could turn into cats. They also believed that cats were witches' 'familiars', or supernatural animal guides that could help them make magic spells.

In Ireland a black cat brings good luck. But in some states of America it is good luck if a black cat visits your house, but bad luck if it stays!

Cats in Children's Books

Bestselling Irish children's writer, Judi Curtin is a huge cat lover. Her own cat, Domino, appears in several of her books.

Jacqueline Wilson once wrote a book called **The Cat Mummy** about a girl who tries to mummify her dead pet cat. Don't try it – it does not work!

Bagheera in **The Jungle Book** is a black panther – which is actually a leopard. How? Its markings are hidden in its dark fur. If you look very carefully at its coat or use an infra-red camera you can make out its spots!

Weird and Wonderful Cats

The Turkish Van loves to swim. It comes from an area around Lake Van in Turkey and is white with brown ears and tail.

The caracal has black pointy ears that stick up and have tufts of hair on the top. They may look cute, but they hunt adult antelope (up to about 50kg). Caracal only weigh 10-20kg so that's about three times their own size!

The Devon rex cat has curly hair and the sphynx has no hair at all!

Manx cats have no tails. They originally came from the Isle of Man, which is where they get their name. Japanese bobtails have a short fluffy tail like a rabbit's.

Eyes and Tongues

Cats' eyes glow in the dark. They have a special layer of reflective cells in their eyes called tapetum lucidum which helps them see in dim light. It also makes their eyes shine in cars' headlights! Did you know that the reflective glass marbles set into road markings to help drive the middle of the road in the dark are also called cats' eyes?

Cats are very clean and love washing themselves. Their tongues are full of spines called 'papillae', which help take meat off bones and are also used for combing their fur. If a big cat licks you, watch out! Its tongue spines feel like rough sandpaper on your skin.

Do Cats Really Have 9 Lives?

Cats are said to have nine lives as they often fall from great heights without hurting themselves.

This isn't true – like all animals, they only have one life! However, many wildcats spend their lives in trees so they need to have brilliant balance. They have adapted to be able to flip their bodies around super quickly and land on their feet – pet cats can do this too!

Hoppy's Feline Facts

🐾 Every cat in the world has a different pattern on its nose pad. Humans have unique fingerprints, cats have unique nose swirls!

🐾 The furry, tufty bits on the inside of cats' ears are called 'ear furnishings'.

🐾 Cats' claws are made of keratin, a protein also found in human nails. All cats apart from cheetahs put away, or sheath, their claws when they are relaxed or running.

🐾 I'm sure you know a baby cat is called a kitten. But did you know that a male cat is called a tom? Or a female cat is called a molly or a queen?

How to Draw a Cat

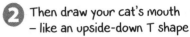

1 First, draw your cat's button nose

2 Then draw your cat's mouth – like an upside-down T shape

3 Next, draw your cat's furry eyebrows

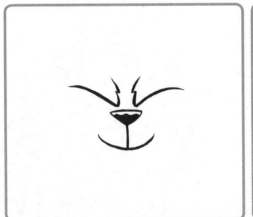

4 Now, draw your cat's eyes – remember to put the little sparkle in!

5 Next up, draw your cat's furry chin

6 Then draw the sides and top of your cat's head – leaving room for...

7 ...the big, furry, triangle-shaped ears

8 Finally, add in some whiskers and, voila, here's your cat! MIAOW!

Ah! C'est magnifique!

The Brilliant World of Horses

Humans and horses have lived and worked together for over four thousand years. Horses have been used to travel long distances, pull carts and wagons, to help on ranches and farms, and even to help soldiers in battle. There are more than three hundred different breeds of horses on the planet.

Today they are still used for farming, transport and also to help police around the world including our own police force, An Garda Síochána. The Gardaí have a mounted support unit based in the Phoenix Park.

In ancient Greece, horse racing was part of the Olympic Games and the people rode without saddles – that must have been tricky! Horses and riders still compete in the Olympics to this day.

Horses are built for running and speed, with long legs, large lungs and strong muscles. In the past this helped them outrun danger in the wild. It has also helped them spread all over the world as they have moved over land from country to country.

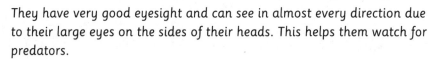
They have very good eyesight and can see in almost every direction due to their large eyes on the sides of their heads. This helps them watch for predators.

Horses are herbivores, which means they eat grass, leaves and shoots. They have flat, wide teeth that help them chew up their food.

Hoofing It

Like deer, cattle, camels, gazelle and even hippos, horses are hoofed mammals or 'ungulates'. Their hooves are made of keratin, the same material that makes up our fingernails! This never stops growing. We have to cut our nails, but animal's hooves wear down as they walk and run. Horns are also made of keratin, but antlers are made of bone.

Domestic horses wear metal horseshoes on their hooves to keep their feet protected on roads. These are fitted by a person called a farrier.

That's zedonk-ulous!

Hoppy's Horsey Facts

When donkeys are bred with zebras they make an animal with a brown coat and narrow stripes. This fine fellow is called a zedonk!

Horses and zebras have one toe on each hoof, cattle and deer have two, rhinos have three toes and hippos have four.

What's the Difference Between a Horse and a Pony?

The answer is size! Horses and ponies are in the same group of animals, but ponies are smaller. If a horse is less than 14.2 hands (148 cm) tall at the base of his neck (called his 'withers') he is a pony.

Ponies tend to be stocky and strong.

Some horses are also bred to be small – these are called miniature horses.

Mules

Mules have a horse mother and a donkey father. Mules are strong and have great stamina, they can walk and walk and carry heavy loads. Have you ever been called 'as stubborn as a mule'? They are known for digging their heels in when they don't want to do something and that's where the phrase comes from!

Wild Horses

There are more than fifty-eight million horses in the world, but the only truly wild species is the endangered Przewalski's horse. By the 1960s this small brown horse could only be found in zoos, but now some specially bred herds have been reintroduced into the grasslands of Mongolia.

Hotbloods and Coldbloods

The terms 'hotblood' or 'coldblood' have nothing to do with the actual temperature of a horse's blood – they describe the horse's temperament, or behaviour.

Hotbloods are horses originally from hot countries like the Middle East or Africa. They are slim and fast and make great racehorses. They can be energetic and nervous.

Coldbloods are horses originally from the colder climates of northern Europe. These horses tend to be heavy and strong and are good for farm work. They are often described as calm and patient.

Sometimes hotbloods are bred with coldbloods to form – you got it – warmbloods! These horses are both fast and strong – a good combination!

Connemara Ponies

These ponies are brilliant at jumping and cross country competitions. They originally came from Ireland, but are now much loved all over the world.

Hoppy's Horsey Facts

There are cave drawings of horses that date back 17,000 years. The most famous are in the Lascaux cave in France.

The white markings on horses or pony's feet are called 'socks'. If the socks go higher than the horse's knee, they are called 'stockings'!

Points of a Horse

The 'points' or parts of a horse are the different bits you can see – and each part has a special name.

If you ride or look after horses you will know all the different points – from the fetlock to the muzzle.

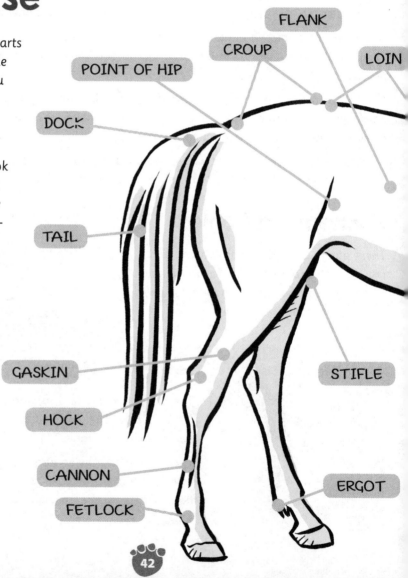

FLANK

CROUP

POINT OF HIP

LOIN

DOCK

TAIL

GASKIN

STIFLE

HOCK

CANNON

ERGOT

FETLOCK

POLL

WITHERS

CREST

SHOULDER

FOREHEAD

BACK

MUZZLE

CHIN GROOVE

THROAT LATCH

ELBOW

FOREARM

That horse makes a lot of good points!

ARREL

CHESTNUT

KNEE

PASTERN

CORONET

HEEL

HOOF

Horse Records

Big and Small

The biggest horses on the planet are Shire horses. The tallest on record stands 198cm from shoulder feet: that's pretty big!

The smallest horse is the Falabella who grows to about 75cm from shoulder to feet – as small as some breeds of dog. They are too small for most people to ride, but are friendly and clever and often kept as pets.

Horses are measured in 'hands' – from their shoulder to the ground. One hand is about 10cm.

How tall are YOU in hands?

1 HAND = 10cm

so...

11 HANDS = 110cm

Oldest Horse

Most horses live for about thirty years, depending on their size and breed. The oldest horse on record was an English horse in the 1700s called Old Billy who lived to be sixty-two.

How to Tell a Horse's Age

Vets look in a horse's mouth and study their teeth to find out how old they are. A horse's front teeth change shape as they get older.

Fastest Horses

Racehorses are bred to be fast and they can gallop at speeds of up to 70km/h.

Famous Irish Racehorses

Arkle was one of the most famous Irish racehorses ever. He won the Cheltenham Gold Cup three years in row, the Irish Grand National and two Hennessy Gold Cups and was voted as the all-time favourite racehorse in Britain and Ireland by the Racing Post newspaper. To this day you can see his skeleton at the Irish Horse Racing Museum.

Other famous racehorses that are called 'Living Legends' include Beef or Salmon, Hardy Eustace, Hurricane Fly, Kicking King, and Rite Of Passage. What brilliant names! These horses are now retired and all live at the Irish National Stud where you can visit them.

Shergar was another famous Irish racehorse. He was worth over 15 million pounds! Back in 1983 he was kidnapped from his stable in Co. Kildare and a ransom was demanded. But this was never paid and to this day no one knows what happened to poor Shergar. Where did he go? Was he shipped abroad? We will never know.

Rainbow Colours

Horses and ponies come in lots of different colours. These have special names. Learn them and you can sound like a horse expert!

CHESTNUT = reddish-gold

SKEWBALD = patches of white and brown

PALOMINO = golden with a white mane and tail

BAY = reddish-brown

DARK BAY = Darker brown

DUN = sandy brown

GREY = from pure white to greyish white

LET'S PLAY HORSES FOR COURSES!

Your horse won't jump the fence, miss a turn!

Your horse stops to pose for a photo, move back 1 square

YOU WILL NEED:

- 2 different coloured counters
- A die

Your horse stumbles, miss a turn!

Your horse won't jump the fence, miss a turn!

START

48

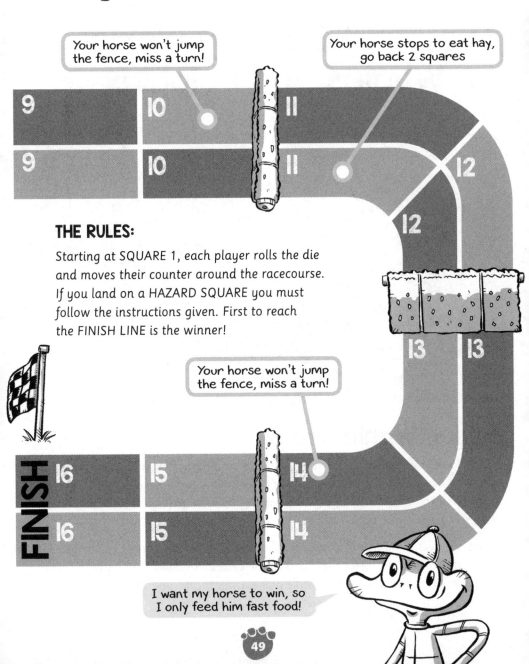

The Mind-Blowing World of Whales and Dolphins

Sarah has a passion for whales and has seen them in Ireland and New Zealand. They are fascinating creatures. Want to find out more – read on!

Which Whale Am I?

Whales are mammals, just like dogs, cats, horses and humans. They are found in seas and oceans all over the world. Some like cold water – narwhals mostly swim in waters around Greenland, Canada and Russia. Beluga whales love the Arctic waters – brrr!

There are over 80 different species of whale – dolphins and porpoises are also types of whale – and they are all part of the cetacean family. Whales with teeth are called 'toothed whales' (scientific name, Odontoceti) and use their teeth to catch and eat fish and other food.

Baleen whales (scientific name, Mysticeti) don't have teeth; instead they have large plates of hairy bristles in their mouths called 'baleen'.

Baleen whales swim along with their mouths open to feed and swallow up huge mouthfuls of water. They then close their mouths and push the water out through the baleen. The food is trapped inside. Isn't that clever?

Humpback whales and blue whales are baleen whales. Blue whales can eat up to 35 million krill every day. Krill are tiny orange sea animals that look like shrimp.

Hoppy's Fun Fin Facts

- Toothed whales are usually smaller than baleen whales. Toothed whales have one blowhole, baleen whales have two.

- Dolphins and porpoises are toothed whales.

- Some baleen whales have large folds or pleats of skin called 'throat grooves', which run from below their mouths to their stomachs. These folds expand during feeding so they can fit even more fish into their mouths. These whales are called rorqual whales. Humpback whales are rorqual whales.

Song of the Sea

Whales use sound to communicate underwater. Baleen whales make low sounds that travel long distances through the water to other whales. The complex and beautiful song of the humpback whale can travel hundreds of kilometres through the water to other humpbacks.

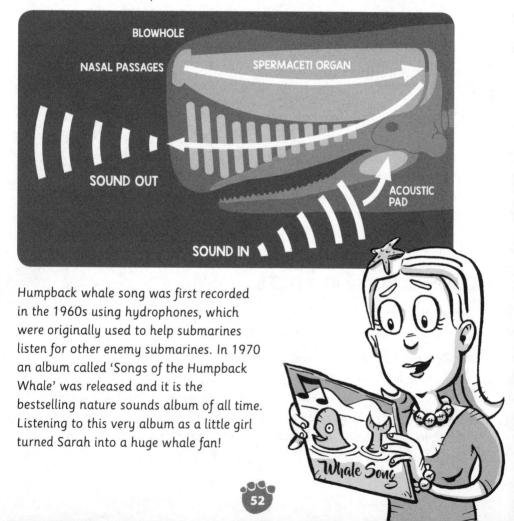

Humpback whale song was first recorded in the 1960s using hydrophones, which were originally used to help submarines listen for other enemy submarines. In 1970 an album called 'Songs of the Humpback Whale' was released and it is the bestselling nature sounds album of all time. Listening to this very album as a little girl turned Sarah into a huge whale fan!

Whale Records

Largest Cetacean: Blue whale.

Can reach 33m in length.

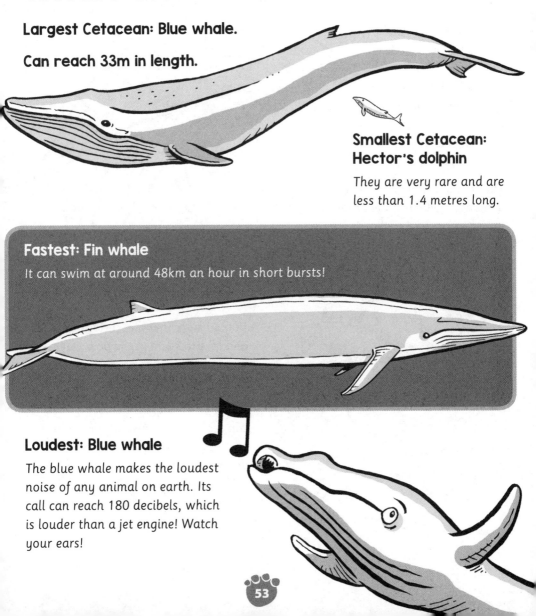

Smallest Cetacean: Hector's dolphin

They are very rare and are less than 1.4 metres long.

Fastest: Fin whale

It can swim at around 48km an hour in short bursts!

Loudest: Blue whale

The blue whale makes the loudest noise of any animal on earth. Its call can reach 180 decibels, which is louder than a jet engine! Watch your ears!

We Are Family

Most toothed whales live in groups called schools or pods. The pods vary in size from two to more than fifty whales. Sometimes dolphin pods are made up of over a thousand animals!

They make an amazing sight swimming and jumping together in the ocean. Jumping out of the water is called 'porpoising', even when dolphins are doing it.

Dolphins are friendly, curious animals and love to swim in the bow waves of boats. Porpoises are shy and live alone or in small groups.

Dolphins are super intelligent. They can recognise themselves in a mirror and can mimic a human or another dolphin. As their intelligence is very different to ours, scientists are only starting to understand how clever they really are!

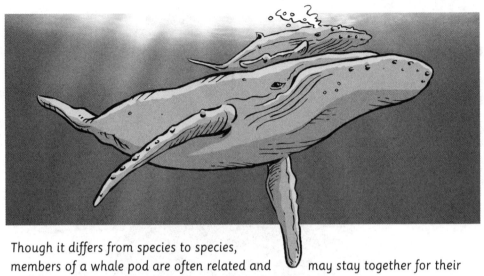

Though it differs from species to species, members of a whale pod are often related and may stay together for their whole lives. Baby whales are called calves; they stay with their mothers for at least two or three years as they grow and learn about the ocean. They sometimes rest their flippers on their mother's side to help them swim or when they get tired, like a toddler might hold its mum or dad's hand when learning to walk!

Hoppy's Fun Fin Facts

- Every dolphin in the world has its own signature whistle. It's like their fingerprint or their name. If they want to call out to another dolphin they can do this by using the other dolphin's signature whistle – the way you might call your friend's name! They are the only other animal in the planet that can do this – that we know of!

- Pink dolphins are real! They are called botos and live in the Amazon and Orinoco river basins in Bolivia, Brazil, Colombia, Ecuador, Guyana, Peru, and Venezuela.

Take a deep breath...

Like all mammals, whales and dolphins have to breathe air. Sperm whales can stay underwater for ninety minutes, humpback whales about thirty minutes, while dolphins need to breathe every ten or fifteen minutes. It's why you see dolphins popping up to breathe much more than whales. It also means that if dolphins get caught up in fishing nets they can drown.

Dolphins have to be conscious to breathe. This means that they cannot go into a full deep sleep, so instead they shut down half their brain – the scientific name for this is – wait for it – uni-hemispheric sleeping.

Whaling was banned in 1986, but some countries still hunt whales. Many whales such as blue whales are endangered because of hunting. Today there are only 10,000 to 25,000 blue whales in the oceans.

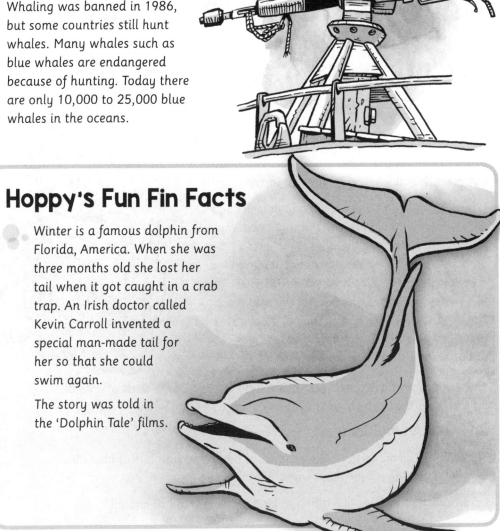

Hoppy's Fun Fin Facts

Winter is a famous dolphin from Florida, America. When she was three months old she lost her tail when it got caught in a crab trap. An Irish doctor called Kevin Carroll invented a special man-made tail for her so that she could swim again.

The story was told in the 'Dolphin Tale' films.

PART 2

Evolution or How Animals Became So Cool

Evolution and the Animal Tree

The wonderful world of evolution. A dollop of science for all you super-smart girls and boys out there to make you even super smarter!

Life on earth began around 3.8 billion years ago with teeny, tiny living things that only had one cell. Over millions of years these single cells gradually evolved, or slowly changed, into more complex life forms. This is called EVOLUTION. In 1859 a man called Charles Darwin wrote a book called On the Origin of Species all about evolution. Scientists are still fascinated by evolution and study it to this day.

There are currently around two million different species or kinds of animals on planet earth. More about the different species in a moment.

First – **The Animal Tree**

The story of life on earth is often shown as a big tree with lots of branches and twigs coming off the main trunk.

Each branch of the tree is a different kind of living thing or animal.

The Animal Tree

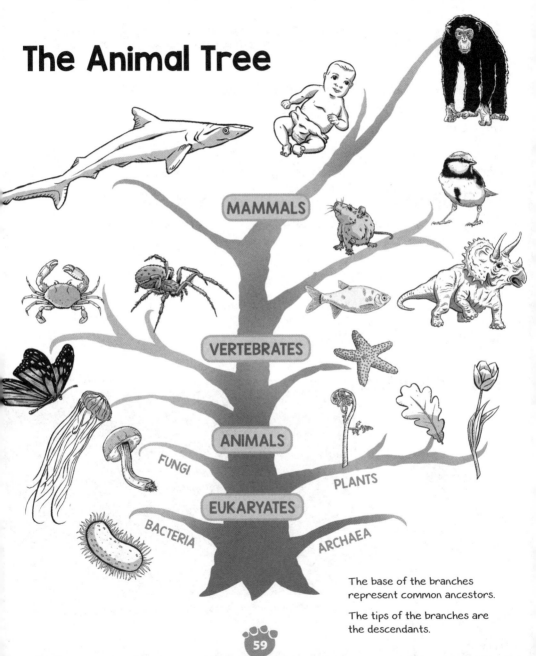

MAMMALS

VERTEBRATES

ANIMALS

FUNGI

PLANTS

EUKARYATES

BACTERIA

ARCHAEA

The base of the branches
represent common ancestors.

The tips of the branches are
the descendants.

Who Am I? Animal Species

There are around two million different animal species on earth THAT WE KNOW OF. Scientists believe that there could be as many as 6 or even 7 million out there, waiting to be found. New species are being discovered all the time.

Around 95 per cent of all animals are

INVERTEBRATES

Or animals with NO back bone – like insects.

The other 5 per cent are

VERTEBRATES

Or animals with backbones

There are 5 main groups of vertebrates:

 Fish Amphibians Reptiles

 Birds Mammals

Amphibians

Amphibians make up around 10% of all vertebrates.

This is what amphibians have in common:

We are cold-blooded (this is also called ectothermic – our body temperatures vary depending on our habitat. Ecto means 'outside' and therm means 'heat')

We lay eggs

We live in water and on land – we need to be moist to stay alive so we like to live in wet places. We can breathe on land or underwater – aren't we cool?

Mammals

Humans are mammals, and mammals make up almost 10 per cent of vertebrates. As of 2018, there are 6,495 species of currently recognized mammals (96 of which are recently extinct).

This is what mammals have in common:

Mammals are warm blooded (or endothermic – they control their own body temperature internally and stay roughly the same temperature in any habitat, warm or cold).

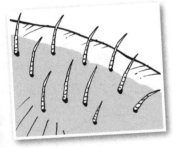

Mammals have hair or fur.

Human skin is covered in tiny hairs; most adult humans have over 5 million hairs on their body! Their ancestors may have been a lot hairier – they needed it to keep them warm, but humans have clothes to keep them cosy now. In fact, human hair helps keep people cool, not warm, as it shades them from the sun.

Mammals breathe oxygen.

Most mammals give birth to live young and feed their babies with their own milk.

Hoppy's Fun Facts

There are two mammals in the world who lay eggs. These are called 'monotremes'. Can you guess their names?

ANSWERS: THE PLATYPUS AND THE ECHIDNA

Birds, Reptiles and Fish

Birds

Birds make up around 20 per cent of vertebrates. There are over 9,800 known species of bird in the world.

They are warm-blooded and lay eggs and are the only animals with feathers.

They have two legs and two wings, but not all birds can fly!

Reptiles

Reptiles make up around 15 per cent of the vertebrates. There are over 7,700 known species of reptiles in the world.

They are cold-blooded and have scales.

Most of them lay eggs and live on land.

They have either four legs or no legs (like snakes).

Fish

Fish make up around a whopping 45 per cent of the vertebrates – that's a lot of swimming! There are over 30,000 known species of fish in the world.

They are cold-blooded and lay eggs.

They breathe oxygen from the water through special organs called gills.

But vertebrates only make up about
5 per cent of the animal kingdom! The other 95 per cent are invertebrates.

Let's find out more about our backbone-less friends!

No (Back) Bones on Us! Invertebrates

Scientists think there may be millions of invertebrates out there just waiting to be discovered. New ones are being discovered all the time.

Invertebrates are: arthropods (which include insects), annelids (like earth worms), molluscs (like slugs and snails), echinoderms (like starfish), cnidarians (like jellyfish), flatworms, comb jellies (which look like oval jellyfish), nematodes (or roundworms) and sponges. Lots of interesting words there! Let's find out more about some of them:

Arthropods

The bodies of arthropods are made up of different sections and are covered by a hard shell called an exoskeleton, which protects them. They are like tiny super heroes with built-in battle armour on the outside!

They have six or more legs.

85 per cent of the world's animals are anthropods.

Crabs are anthropods, as well as centipedes, spiders and insects.

There are over 900,000 different known species of insects on the earth – that's a lot of creepy crawlies!

Annelids – Segmented Worms and Round Worms

Annelids have no legs, their bodies are made up of different segments.

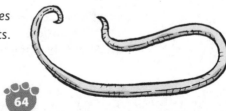

Molluscs

Molluscs are animals like squid, slugs, snails and octopi (the plural of octopus). They don't have legs, but some (like the octopus and squid) have tentacles.

They have a soft, squishy body and most have a shell either inside or outside their body. They die if they dry up so are mostly found in or near water. A few molluscs like slugs and snails have adapted to live on land.

Echinoderms

Echinoderms have no heart, eyes or brain, but their skin is sensitive to temperature, light and the movement of the air or sea around them.

Sea urchins and starfish are echinoderms.

Cnidarians

Jellyfish and sea anemones are cnidarians – these animals have tentacles that sting and sack-like bodies.

Flatworms have soft, flat bodies.

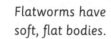

Sponges don't have any organs, but they have holes all over them that let in oxygen and food.

Wow – so many invertebrates!

What's in a Name?

Hi, everyone!

Tree frogs like me are part of the Hylidae family of frogs.

Happy Hylidae, Everyone!

Sorry, bad joke!

My two-part scientific name is: wait for it, it's a bit of a mouthful: Agalychnis callidryas

AGALYCHNIS CALLIDRYAS

All animals have a scientific name and all scientific names have two parts — like a human's first name and surname.

The first part tells people my 'genus': 'Agalychnis' is a type of tree frog. It also tells people where I'm from: Forests in Mexico, Central America and north-western South America.

And the second part tells you a bit more about me – in my case, 'Callidryas' comes from the Greek words 'kallos', meaning beautiful, and 'dryas' meaning tree nymph.

I like that! I'm a beautiful tree nymph!

In fact, no two living things have the same scientific name, but most animals are known by their 'common' name.

Here are some more scientific names:

Killer whales – Orcinus Orca

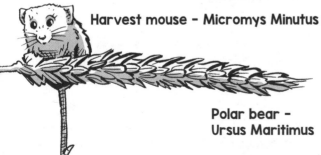

Harvest mouse – Micromys Minutus

Polar bear – Ursus Maritimus

Dinosaurs and Early Animals

For around 160 million years, dinosaurs ruled the earth. Dinosaurs were huge reptiles, much bigger than any animals today.

Scientists know about dinosaurs from fossils.

What are Fossils?

Fossils are a record of animals and plants that lived a long time ago. They are usually the remains of the hard parts of an animal, like its bones or shell. They are found in rocks.

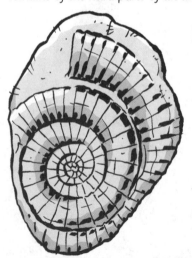

How are Fossils Formed?

When animals die, their bodies sink into the ground or the mud or sand on the sea floor. The soft parts of their bodies rot away, but the hard parts remain.

The sediment – the mud or sand – covers the remaining hard parts and slowly turns into rock. The fossils are trapped in the rock, waiting to be found.

Fossils give us clues about animals from the past. A 'paleontologist' is a scientist who studies fossils.

Hoppy's Fun Fossil Fact

Mary Anning from Dorset, England was only twelve in 1811 when she found the skeleton of an Ichthyosaurus, a large marine animal from the Jurassic period.

Hoppy's Fun Fossil Fact

The youngest person to discover a fossil of an unknown dinosaur was Diego Suarez from Chile. He was only seven in 2004 when he found pieces of vertebrae from a prehistoric creature in the ground. Scientists named the dinosaur Chilesaurus diegosuarezi in his honour.

Hoppy's Fun Fossil Fact

Looking for fossils is fun! In Ireland you might find small fossils in the limestone of Doolin Pier in Co. Clare. Or you can see little footprints of an ancient animal called a Tetrapod (which looked like a large lizard) on the Valentia Trackway, Co. Kerry. Scientists think the prints are at least 365 million years old – that's ancient! Keep your eyes open if you're on an Irish beach – you never know what you might spot hidden in the rocks!

Dinosaurs

Dinosaur Timeline

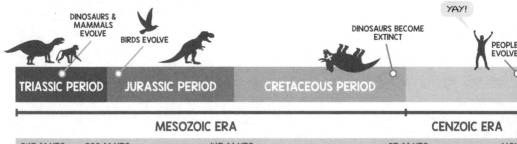

Dinosaurs roamed the earth between about 245 and 66 million years ago, in a time known as the Mesozoic Era. This era is split into three periods; Triassic, Jurassic and Cretaceous. Dinosaurs lived through all three.

During this time the first birds evolved from small, feathery dinosaurs and modern sharks and early amphibians started to appear.

Between 145 and 65 million years ago giant meat-eating dinosaurs like the Tyrannosaurus Rex appeared. The Cretaceous period was also when many species of animals, including the dinosaurs died out. Scientists think Earth was hit by a giant asteroid, which threw up clouds of dust and changed the climate. The animals who survived were the ones who were able to adapt to the new conditions.

Insects, fish, birds, worms and mammals all survived and their descendants are still alive today.

The early ancestors of humans appeared around 5 million years ago.

Modern humans like you – Homo sapiens – only emerged 300,000 years ago.

Diplodocus

The Diplodocus lived around 150 million years ago. It was a giant plant-eating dinosaur with a very long neck and tail. Their necks were three times as long as a giraffe's neck and at a whopping 12 tonnes they weighed up to four times as much as a modern elephant.

But they had very small heads – about the same size as a modern horse's head! They used their tail to scare off predators. When they cracked their tail like a whip it could be heard for many kilometres.

They ate ferns and leaves and lived to the ripe old age of eighty. The fossil skeleton of a young Diplodocus was discovered in Wyoming, America in 2011. The scientists called it 'Twinky'.

Tyrannosaurus Rex

At 6 metres high, the Tyrannosaurus or T-Rex was one of the largest meat-eating animals on earth.

It was a pretty scary animal too! It had huge, powerful jaws designed to crush bones and sharp teeth in the shape of cones that could rip through flesh.

Scientists think it could eat over 200kg of meat in one bite – that's like chewing and swallowing a large pig in one go!

Early Mammals – Woolly Mammoths

Woolly mammoth bodies over 20,000 years old have been found buried in ice. They lived in Russia, Asia and North America during the Ice Age when the world was covered in snow and ice, long, long after the time of the dinosaurs.

They had a thick coat and a thick layer of fat under their skin to keep them warm. In 1994 scientists found genetic material called DNA in the fossil remains of a woolly mammoth. They discovered that the DNA was almost identical to the DNA of modern elephants.

The Columbian mammoth was even bigger than the woolly mammoth and lived in North America and Mexico. It had a smoother coat as it lived in warmer places. It weighed over ten tonnes – the weight of 160 adult humans!

Draw a Dino!

1 Start with the dinosaur's eyes and eyebrows

4 Next, draw the dinosaur's back and tail

That drawing is dino-mite!

2 Add the nose and mouth

3 Draw the dino's nostrils and big, sharp teeth

5 Now, draw the front arms and tummy

6 Finish off by drawing the legs – RRAAWWRR!

Ah! C'est magnifique!

Now You See Me, Now You Don't – Animal Camouflage

Many animals use camouflage to hide themselves in their surroundings. This allows them to disappear. Predators can't see them and they can also creep up on their own prey. Sneaky, eh?

When zebras move together in a herd their bold stripes mask movement, confusing predators about the direction and speed of the herd (it only works when they are moving, but it makes it hard for a predator to pick an individual target). This is called 'motion dazzle'.

Razzle dazzle them, I say!

Tigers use camouflage too. Their stripy pattern helps them blend into the tall, wavy grass on the savannah. This is called 'disruptive colouration'.

The colours of sandpiper chicks and their eggs match their nests so cleverly that they can't be seen. This is called 'cryptic colouring'.

And some animals can change their skin colour or pattern to exactly match their background – how clever is that? Fish, reptiles, octopus and frogs do this.

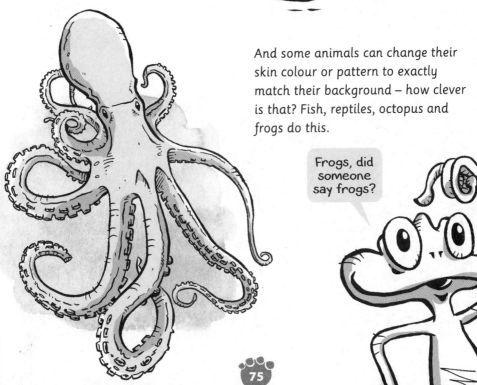

75

Smooth Operators – Animal Camouflage

Other animals hide themselves in clever ways too. Stick insects lie still and look just like twigs on a tree.

Leaf mantis insects look just like leaves. Some species have even adapted to look like dead leaves!

This is called 'mimesis' – basically they are 'miming' being something else – in this case a twig or a leaf.

Animals really are masters of disguise!

Can you see me?
I'm in this tree!

Beware!

Some animals use colour and patterns to warn predators that they are dangerous or disgusting to eat. This is called 'aposematism'.

Poison dart frogs come in various colourations. Their colouring can be yellow, gold, copper, red, green, blue, or black with various patterns – they all taste pretty nasty.

Skunks have a very distinctive black and white fur – and boy, do they smell disgusting if they feel they are under attack and waft their evil-smelling odour in your direction!

The blue-ringed octopus may look beautiful with its yellow colouring and bright blue rings, but its deadly bite can kill a human in less than fifteen minutes. Luckily it's mostly found in coral reefs in the Pacific or Indian Oceans and not on Irish beaches!

 **PART 3**

Animal Record Breakers

Big and Small

Animals come in all shapes and sizes.

The largest animal on the whole planet is the blue whale. It can grow to 33 metres, that's the length of three and a half double decker buses!

It can weigh up to 180 tonnes or the weight of fifty-five hippopotami.

Its heart is the size of a small car, like a Mini. It has the largest heart of any animal in the world.

And it could fit fifty people in its huge mouth. But don't worry, it doesn't eat children, mainly just tiny shrimp-like sea animals called krill – 40 million of them a day!

The smallest mammal is Kitti's hog-nosed bat, which is only 3cm long and weighs less than a 1 cent coin.

2.8m

The largest bird is the ostrich at 2.8m tall.

The smallest is the male bee hummingbird at around 6cm long.

Big and Small

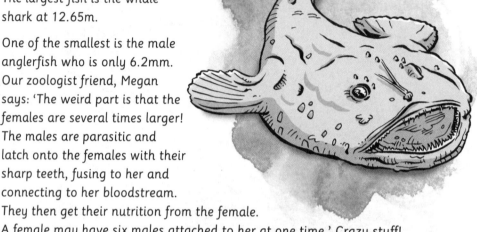

The largest fish is the whale shark at 12.65m.

One of the smallest is the male anglerfish who is only 6.2mm. Our zoologist friend, Megan says: 'The weird part is that the females are several times larger! The males are parasitic and latch onto the females with their sharp teeth, fusing to her and connecting to her bloodstream. They then get their nutrition from the female. A female may have six males attached to her at one time.' Crazy stuff!

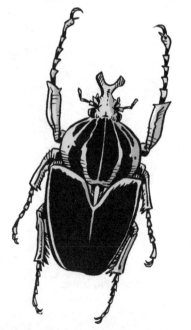

The smallest animal in the whole ocean – and the smallest animal full stop – may be the teeny tiny myxozoa, which is a worm-like creature (a cnidarian like the jellyfish) that lives on fishes' skin. At 0.01mm it's so tiny you almost can't see it!

The largest insect (by weight) is the Goliath beetle which lives in Africa. It can weigh up to 100g or as much as five house mice.

The smallest insect is a kind of fairyfly from Costa Rica which is called Tinkerbell and is a teeny tiny 0.25mm long.

Giant anacondas are the largest reptiles – they can grow up to nine metres long – or as long as a bus.

Imagine meeting one of those in your garden!

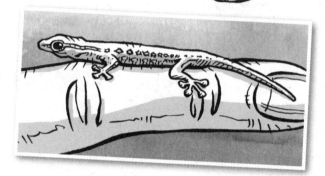

The smallest reptile is the dwarf gecko from the Dominican Republic. It's so small it could easily sit on the tip of your little finger.

What about frogs?

And the smallest is the paedophryne, which at 7mm is so small it can easily sit on your fingernail.

In case you're wondering – I'm 4cm long!

The largest frog is the Goliath frog, which can grow to the same size as a pet cat.

How big are you?

Fast and Slow

The sloth is the slowest animal in the world. The top speed of a sloth is 0.003 miles per hour and they are so slow that plants and algae grow on them. Imagine!

Peregrine falcons are the fastest animals on the planet. They can reach speeds of up to a whizzy 300km/hour while diving down through the sky to catch their prey, making them fearsome hunters.

Cheetahs are the fastest land animals – they can sprint at about 100km/hour – that's fast!

Sail fish are no slouches either. Imagine being speared by one at over 100km/hour – ouch!

How Do Animals Move?

Animals like frogs use their strong back legs to hop around. So do kangaroos and fleas. Fleas can jump up to 200 times their own body length.

Snakes slither along in S-shapes by stretching or flexing different parts of their bodies at the same time. Birds and other winged animals use their wings to fly and glide through the air.

Jellyfish squirt along by pulling water into their bodies and squirting it out fast, like little jet engines. Sea animals use their fins, tails and bodies to push them through the water.

And animals who have legs walk or run. Millipedes have the most legs in the animal kingdom – some as many as a whopping 400 legs. And the Illacme plenipes, a rare millipede from America has around 750 legs – try counting those!

Most Dangerous and Deadly Animals

Most wild animals, even the biggest and boldest, try to avoid contact with humans. But sometimes they can cause harm to people and even kill. However, scary animals like sharks and crocodiles don't kill the most people. In the animal world small can be deadly!

Top five most dangerous animals in the world to humans:

5 Hippos

Hippos are highly territorial and will attack people and crush them with their hefty bodies if they enter their part of the river. They kill around 400 people a year.

4 Crocodiles

Crocodiles kill around 1,000 people a year. They are one of the few wild animals who actively hunt humans for food. The saltwater crocodile has one of the strongest bites in the world – about twenty times stronger than a human bite.

3 Scorpions

Scorpions, like the Indian red scorpion, kill around 3,000 people a year. They are found in Sri Lanka, Nepal, India and Pakistan. They mostly keep themselves hidden, but if they are disturbed they can sting with their tails. Their venom is highly poisonous.

2 Snakes

Snakes like the Indian cobra and the saw-scaled viper kill between 94,000 and 125,000 people a year, according the the World Health Organisation. Cobras pump venom through their fangs and some can even spit venom!

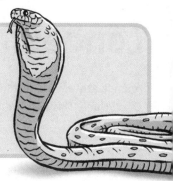

1 Mosquitos

The most dangerous animal in the world is the tiny mosquito. It carries a disease called malaria, which kills up to a million people a year according to UNICEF. It is mainly found in Africa.

Other dangerous animlas include sharks, jellyfish, bees (many people are allergic to bee stings), lions and elephants.

Dogs are also very dangerous in some countries, as they can carry a disease called rabies.

Paws for Thought

The most deadly animal of all, of course, is the human. Humans kill millions of other animals every year through hunting, destroying habitats and pollution.

Hoppy's Fun Facts

🐾 The African rock python is a constrictor – that means it squeezes its prey to death with its incredibly powerful body. It then swallows it whole. Scientists think the squeeze kills by causing a heart attack.

🐾 The golden poison frog is bright yellow and has a highly toxic skin. A single frog has enough poison it its body to kill ten people.

🐾 SURVIVAL TIP: sharks and crocodiles will often let go of their victims after the first bite, so this is the best time to try to escape!

Longest Migrations

Animals travel long distances to find food, find a mate or to raise their babies. Or all three. This is called 'migration'. And some animals travel unbelievable distances.

Leatherback turtles travel up to 16,000km to find tasty jellyfish to eat. They manage to find their way back to the very same beach where they were born to lay their own eggs. That's some journey!

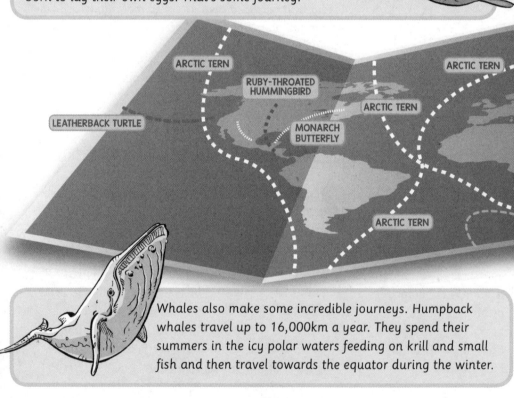

ARCTIC TERN

RUBY-THROATED HUMMINGBIRD

ARCTIC TERN

LEATHERBACK TURTLE

ARCTIC TERN

MONARCH BUTTERFLY

ARCTIC TERN

ARCTIC TERN

Whales also make some incredible journeys. Humpback whales travel up to 16,000km a year. They spend their summers in the icy polar waters feeding on krill and small fish and then travel towards the equator during the winter.

Ruby-throated hummingbirds may look fragile, but they fly around 2,000km a year. In spring they fly to North America and nest, and in the autumn they travel south to sunny Central America.

Monarch butterflies fly almost 5,000km a year from Canada and northern America to Mexico. They spend the winter in the sun, hanging from the trees and sleeping until spring.

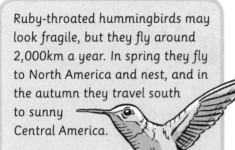

LEATHERBACK TURTLE

HUMPBACK WHALE

ARCTIC TERN

But the migration king is the Arctic tern who travels over 80,000km every year. These small birds fly from the Arctic to the Antarctic every year – seeing more daylight than any other animal on earth and having not one, but two summers! Clever birds!

PART 4
ANIMALS ALL AROUND IRELAND

What is a Native Species?

A native species is an animal or plant that occurs naturally in an area or habitat. They can also be called an 'indigenous species'.

Some animals visit Ireland as they migrate or travel to different countries. The Eurasian woodcock spends the winter in Ireland before flying back to Norway, Sweden or even as far as Russia to breed in the spring.

There are also non-native species (sometimes called an 'introduced' or 'alien' species) – these are species that are not normally found in particular areas, but are still growing or living there. If a non-native species is causing problems to an area then they are called an 'invasive' species.

The grey squirrel is not native to Ireland and is an invasive species because it causes problems to the native red squirrel. The grey squirrel is bigger and takes the red squirrel's space and food. It can also carry a virus that is dangerous to red squirrels.

How many different species of animals are found in Ireland?

There are twenty-four species of sea mammals found in Irish waters – including bottle-nosed dolphins, common dolphins, harbour porpoises, common seals, grey seals and minke whales – and over 500 species of marine fish.

And fifteen native freshwater fish.

Around twenty-six native land mammals; among the best known are foxes, hedgehogs and bats.

Around 450 birds are found in Irish skies.

Plus a whopping 12,000 insects.

Plus 3 amphibians like me – the smooth newt, the natterjack toad and the common European brown frog.

(Hello, cousin!)

HELLO!

A FROGHORN

And only one native terrestrial reptile – the viviparous lizard (also known as the common lizard).

That's a lot of animals!

The National Biodiversity Data Centre stores all the data, or information, about animals that live in or visit Ireland. It also tracks changes – like how many bumblebees have been seen in a certain season.

Six out of twenty-one of our native bumblebee species are in danger of extinction. You can help track these important animals by becoming a bumblebee spotter and send your info to the Data Centre using their website.

www.biodiversityireland.ie

Hoppy's Amazing Animal Facts
Snakes in Ireland? Not So Fast!

The Burren in Co. Clare is home to a strange lizard with no legs called the slow worm. Sometimes people mistake this fellow for a snake.

They have smooth skin with scales that don't overlap. Slow worms eat slugs and worms and spend a lot of their time hiding so are hard to spot!

They can live to the ripe old age of thirty – making them one of the longest living lizards around.

They aren't native to Ireland. The theory is that they were brought here in the 1970s by New Age Travellers – way out, man!

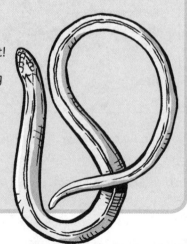

Newts Ahoy!

You can find smooth newts in or around ponds all over Ireland. They are small fellows that look like lizards. They are amphibians like frogs, which means they can live and breathe in the water as well as on land.

They are carnivores – meat eaters – and like to eat small water creatures, spiders, slugs and worms – delicious! Female newts lay their eggs on the leaves of aquatic (water) plants that are growing in a pond. These eggs develop into larvae, or newt tadpoles, which live in the water and have gills, and then develop further into small newts, with legs and lungs, called 'efts'. As adults, newts are mainly terrestrial, as their gills shrink.

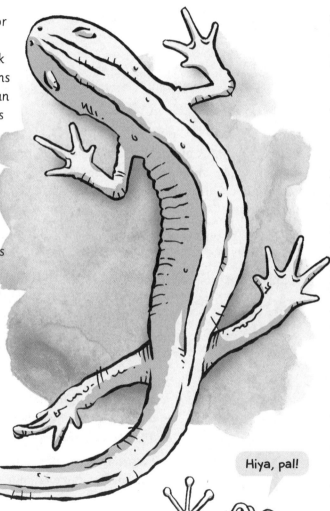

Hiya, pal!

City Slickers

Lots of people live in Dublin city, but did you know that it's also teeming with animal life?

You can find all kinds of animals in every park and garden, on every canal bank and around every corner, you just need to keep your eyes open.

Otters

You may not think of otters as city animals, but they have been spotted along the River Liffey and the River Dodder. They have also been spotted in Cork, Limerick and Galway and other Irish towns and cities. Almost 10,000 of them live in Ireland.

Otters are nocturnal, that means they come out mostly at night. They live beside rivers and mainly eat fish. Sometimes they munch on frogs or rats too!

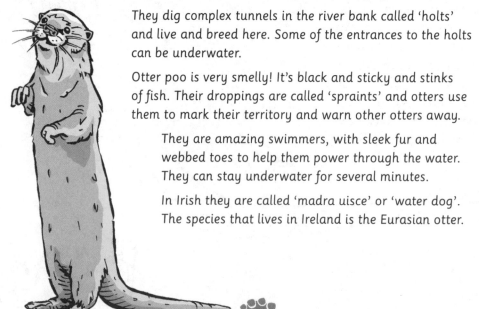

They dig complex tunnels in the river bank called 'holts' and live and breed here. Some of the entrances to the holts can be underwater.

Otter poo is very smelly! It's black and sticky and stinks of fish. Their droppings are called 'spraints' and otters use them to mark their territory and warn other otters away.

They are amazing swimmers, with sleek fur and webbed toes to help them power through the water. They can stay underwater for several minutes.

In Irish they are called 'madra uisce' or 'water dog'. The species that lives in Ireland is the Eurasian otter.

The Red Fox

There are more red foxes in the city than in the countryside as it's easy for them to find food. There are up to 200,000 of them in Ireland, that's a lot of foxes!

Did you know that the fox is actually a wild dog? Its name in Irish is 'madra rua' or 'red dog'.

Like otters, foxes are nocturnal and spend most of the day underground in their den or 'earth'.

They have excellent hearing and use their ears to hunt rats, mice, rabbits and birds. It is often said that they can hear a watch ticking more than thirty metres away!

In the city they are notorious for eating rubbish – hamburgers and chips that have been thrown in the bin. They like a nice takeaway! They are scavengers, which means they eat leftovers.

IRISH ANIMAL DETECTIVE

Have you ever seen a fox in your back garden or running along a road at night? I bet you have!

SPOOKY!

Female foxes are called vixen and male foxes are called dogs. Baby foxes are cubs or kits.

They are generally quiet animals, but sometimes they let out ear-piercing high-pitched shrieks that sound almost like human screams.

Bats

Yum! Insects!

There are nine resident species of bat in Ireland and lots of these live in the city. Bats are mammals and, like otters and foxes, they are nocturnal. They fly around at night looking for insects like midges and moths to gobble up.

Bats use echolocation to find their food.

How Echolocation Works:

The bat sends out a clicking sound.

This sound bounces off the object – hopefully an insect!

The sound then echoes back to the bat.

The bat is able to use this echo to work out what and where the object is. If it's an insect – bingo! It swoops on it and eats its dinner!

One bat can catch up to 3,000 flying insects in one night.

Irish Bats

Leisler's Bat eats mainly moths and beetles and is the largest Irish bat.

Whiskered Bat has long dark-brown shaggy fur.

Common Pipistrelle – our smallest bat, at around 4cm long!

Natterer's Bat likes to fly low over the ground to catch earwigs.

In the winter bats hibernate or sleep in attics of old buildings or in old tree trunks or in caves. They are famous for sleeping and hibernating upside down, hanging on by their claws.

ZZZZzz

How do they do this?

When we relax our muscles our hands open. Bats' claws work the other way around – their natural state is closed claws. They have to tense their muscles to open their claws. So their claws naturally grip a tree trunk or the ledge of a cave when they are relaxed and sleeping.

IRISH ANIMAL DETECTIVE

Bats live in towns and cities all over Ireland, and in our public parks – keep your eyes peeled at night during the summer when they are not hibernating and you just might spot one!

Hoppy's Fun Facts

🐾 Brown rats came to Ireland around 1720 from Eastern Europe and most people think they are a bit of a pest. They eat all kinds of rubbish and scraps and they can carry bacteria which causes a disease called Weil's disease. Dublin has the most rats in Ireland, followed by Cork and Kildare.

🐾 They are excellent at hiding, great at jumping and climbing, and can squeeze through a hole the size of a five cent coin. Clever animals, rats!

Mini Beasts

Under stones, in old tree stumps, even in your house, live the mini beasts of Ireland! Keep your eyes open and you can spot them everywhere.

There are loads of fun songs and rhymes about mini beasts too – see how many you can think of!

Worms

Yum! Worms!

'There's a worm at the bottom of my garden, and his name is Wiggily Woo.'

Worms are really important mini beasts:

They are FOOD for lots of animals like birds and badgers.

They make lots of little tunnels in the soil that let air in and allow water to move around under the ground. This helps plants grow.

They eat bits of old plants and bits of dead animals and put the good stuff – the nutrients – back into the soil in their poo. Worm poo is called castings. They can eat at least a third of their body weight every day.

Worms have soft moist skin, which is made up of segments or rings called annuli. If a worm is damaged or some of its segments are pecked away by a bird they can grow back – that's pretty cool!

Their bodies are supported by a fluid skeleton called a hydrostatic skeleton.

They have five hearts (or aortic arches, which are very like hearts) and breathe oxygen from the soil through their skin. They don't have eyes, ears or a nose – they have taste receptors and light receptors on their skin. They even use their skin to smell.

Worms move by tightening up (or contracting) their muscles – this shortens their body. Then they relax their muscles, which lengthens the body. They have muscles that go around their body (circular muscles) and up and down their body (longitudinal muscles). Tighten, relax, tighten, relax – this moves them along in the soil.

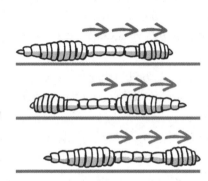

There are twenty-seven species of worm in Ireland, but the common earthworm is the best known. Others include the black head (they have a darker head), the night crawler (they can grow up to 30cm long) and the brandling worm, also known as the tiger worm (they love compost heaps).

Hoppy's Fun Facts

Each segment of a worm's body has small hairs called 'setae', which grip the soil as they burrow. If you put a worm on a dry piece of paper or kitchen roll and listen very carefully you can hear the hairs make little scratchy sounds.

Ladybirds

'Ladybird, Ladybird, fly away home.'

There are around eighteen different kinds of ladybird in Ireland. The best known is the seven-spot ladybird. Most people think ladybirds are cute with their perky, round bodies and red and black backs, but they are monster aphid (greenfly) eaters. That's why gardeners love ladybirds so much – they can eat up to a hundred greenfly a day.

'Greenfly' can actually be black, brown or green – confusing, eh? They are sap-sucking insects who love to eat the fresh new buds on your granny's best rose bushes!

Ladybirds have six legs and usually live for about a year. They lay their eggs on the back of leaves in batches of up to three hundred.

Ladybirds have an interesting life cycle, they develop from legs, to larva, to pupa and then to adult. This is like the life cycle of the butterfly - learn more about that on p 108:

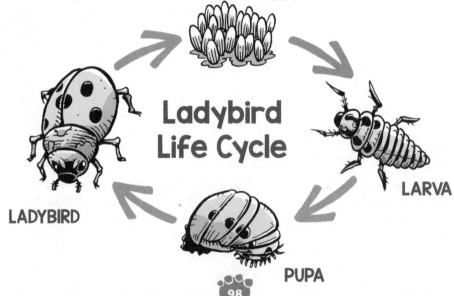

EGGS

Ladybird
Life Cycle

LADYBIRD

LARVA

PUPA

Ladybirds are toxic to predators and are brightly coloured to show other animals that they taste horrible. They also have other defense mechanisms:

They can curl up and pull their legs in, using their hard wing cases to protect them.

They can also leak a liquid from their leg joints that tastes and smells disgusting to put off predators. This is known as 'reflex bleeding'. If you pick up a ladybird you may find an orange liquid on your skin – this is its reflex blood and is full of toxins – warning: never, ever lick it!

YUK!

Spiders

Flies are pretty tasty if you get a nice juicy or crunchy one!

'Incy Wincy spider climbed up the water spout.'

Spiders are carnivores (meat eaters) and eat moths, flies or any small insects they can catch. They have big appetites – one spider might eat 10 per cent of their own weight in small flies every day. They inject venom into their prey before eating them. They are also cannibals – they will eat other spiders.

Spiders are in fact arachnids, not insects. Their animal relations include scorpions. There are over 60,000 different types of arachnids in the world and over 1,100 of these live in Ireland.

Spiders' bodies are made up of two parts and eight legs (insects generally have three body parts and six legs). Even though they have six or eight eyes they don't see all that well. Most spiders only live for one year, but some species like the false widow live for up to six years.

Some spiders make a web to catch their food.

They have silk glands, called 'spinnerets' that produce silk. At the tips of the spinnerets, nozzles (called spigots) shoot out the silk.

The circular webs that look like wheels with lots of inner wheels inside are called orb webs. Each kind of spider weaves a different kind of web.

Hoppy's Fun Facts

 Spider silk is incredibly strong – it's five times stronger than steel of the same thickness. They also use the silk to wrap up egg cocoons. Baby spiders are called spiderlings.

 When spider webs are abandoned we call them cobwebs.

Some spiders found in Ireland are:

SPIDER	WHAT SIZE ARE THEY?	DO THEY BITE?
Daddy Long Legs	45mm	No (or very, very rarely)
Giant House Spiders	120mm	Yes, but they rarely do
Wolf spiders	5 to 8mm	Very, very rarely
Money spiders	2mm	No – they are harmless and some say lucky!
False widow spiders	20mm	Yes – and it hurts! (But it's very rare)

In Your Garden
Robins

Robins live in gardens, woods and forests around Ireland. They love insects and worms, but will also eat seeds and fruit. There are around five million robins in Ireland. The Irish robin species is the European robin; the Irish name for a robin is 'spideog'.

Irish robins are often friendly and hop around when people are gardening, hoping for a worm or insect to be dug up for them. They do this in the wild too, following big animals like deer around and waiting for them to turn up the earth with their hooves. Robins found in other parts of the world can be shy around humans.

Young robins have brown feathers on their chest. They only turn red when they lose their first feathers, which is called moulting.

What is a robin saying when it's singing?

Have you heard a robin singing in your garden? Most singing birds are male and they are using their song to attract females. And also to warn other males not to invade their territory – 'Stay clear of my garden, buster!' they are saying!

If you love birds, check out BirdWatch Ireland and join in on their garden bird surveys.

www.birdwatchireland.ie

Paws for Thought

 Did you know that some birds like sparrows are vegetarians – eating mainly fruit and seeds? In the animal world this is called 'frugivorous' and 'granivorous'.

 Some birds like kingfishers eat only fish – they are called 'piscivorous'.

 And some like bluebirds only eat insects, worms and spiders. They are called 'insectivorous'.

 You can also find blackbirds, blue tits, goldfinches, greenfinches and chaffinches in your garden.

Hedgehogs

Hedgehogs are mammals. They are carnivores and eat slugs, snails, spiders, caterpillars, worms, fruit and all kinds of insects. They travel up to 3km every night looking for food and often visit gardens searching for tasty treats. They have also been known to eat from dog bowls!

The Irish for hedgehog is 'gráinneog'. Baby hedgehogs are called hoglets. The type of hedgehog we have in Ireland is the Western European hedgehog.

Hedgehogs are covered in over 4,000 prickly spines. These protect them from predators like foxes, owls and badgers. When they are threatened they curl up in a ball, making their spines point out.

They are nocturnal – which means you mostly spot them at night. In Ireland they are often knocked down by cars.

This way, lads!

In Ancient Egypt and in the Middle Ages people used to eat roasted hedgehogs. Their meat is still eaten in some parts of the world and their quills and meat are also used in traditional medicine in some African countries.

Like bats, hedgehogs hibernate in the winter. Hibernation is when animals go into a deep sleep so that they can save energy and survive without eating, living off their own body fat. Their heart rate and temperature both go down. A hedgehog's heartbeat drops from over 200 beats a minute to around twenty beats a minute.

Hedgehogs usually hibernate from October or November until late March or April. They build a kind of nest to hibernate in (called a hibernaculum) in roots of trees, under hedges, in compost heaps and under sheds.

Butterflies

There are thirty-three different species of butterfly native to Ireland and many of them are very beautiful.

Butterflies have six legs and large wings compared to their body size; these beat around twenty times a second to keep them in the air.

Their feelers or antennae help them to find food.

They have a long tube instead of a mouth. This is called a 'proboscis'. They stick it into a flower and suck up the nectar – delicious!

Butterflies can only drink liquid food.

Hoppy's Flutter Facts

 Nectar is a sugary liquid produced by plants. They produce it to attract animals like butterflies and bees who then pick up pollen on their bodies when sucking nectar and bring it to other plants helping with pollination.

 Pollination: the transfer of pollen from the male part of the plant to the female part which helps create seeds.

Butterflies use camouflage to hide themselves – the patterns on their wings help them blend in to the plants and landscape and hide from predators like birds and rats (which pretty much eat anything!).

They have been around for a whopping 56 million years – that's a lot of ancestors!

If you'd like to see more butterflies in your garden, plant a wild area or leave an area wild until late autumn, so butterflies have plenty of plants to lay their eggs on. You could also plant daisies, lavender and marigolds as butterflies love the nectar from these flowers.

Butterfly Life Cycle

Butterflies start as little eggs, which are attached to a plant with a fast-drying glue-like chemical that the female produces. Isn't nature clever?

If you look hard enough (or have a magnifying glass) you can see a tiny caterpillar inside the eggs of some butterfly species – isn't that cool?

The eggs hatch into tiny caterpillars. They start eating the leaves of the plant they hatched onto.

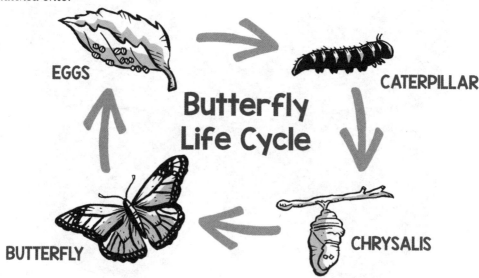

The caterpillars eat and eat and grow and grow. They form a papery shell or case around themselves (sometimes called a cocoon) and turn into what's called a pupa or chrysalis.

After about two weeks of amazing change and transformation the caterpillars turn into butterflies.

It really is one of the most magical transformations of the animal kingdom!

Butterflies found in Irish gardens include:

PEACOCK

RED ADMIRAL

PAINTED LADY

Butterfly Art

1 Fold over your paper and paint half a colourful butterfly

2 Fold your paper back over itself and press down with your hands

You will need:

 A paintbrush

 Some poster paints

 Some paper

3 Open up the paper to find a beautiful butterfly!

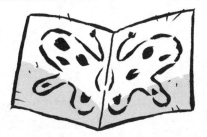

Oh, I Do Like to Be Beside the Seaside!

Lots of Irish animals live beside or in the sea. We've already found out about some of our ocean mammal friends around the world. These sea mammals are native to Irish waters:

 Grey seals

 Common seals

 Common dolphins

 Bottle-nosed dolphins (like Fungie from Dingle)

 Harbour porpoises

 Minke whales

Let's meet two of them!

Minke Whales

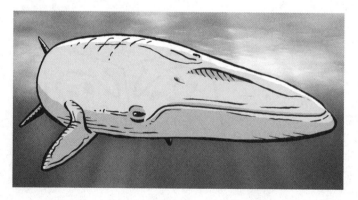

Minke whales are the largest sea mammals that you will see in the Irish Sea. Other whales like humpbacks and orcas or killer whales can sometimes be seen in the Atlantic Ocean to the west of the country.

Grey Seal

The common seal and the grey seal both live in Ireland. Confusingly, there are more grey seals than common seals! Ireland regularly supports about 7,000 to 9,000 grey seals and over 2,000 common seals.

Female seals are called cows, male seals are called bulls and baby seals are called pups. Seals belong to a group of mammals called 'pinnipeds', which means 'wing-footed', and also includes sealions and walruses. There are thirty-three kinds of pinnipeds around the world.

Seals are warm-blooded and have a thick layer of fat under their skin to keep them insulated against the cold sea. This is called blubber. They also have fur all over their bodies to keep them cosy. Their smooth, long shape is ideal for swimming fast.

They hunt for food underwater and use their sensitive whiskers or 'vibrissae' to feel or sense fish or other prey. Their eyes have adapted to see in the dim underwater light and their nostrils close when they are underwater.

They eat mainly fish, octopus and squid and can stay underwater for up to thirty minutes. They can also sleep while they are in the water. They float with their heads sticking up so they can breathe. This is called 'bottling'.

Grey seal pups are born in the autumn; their fur is off-white when they are born. They stay on land for the first six weeks of their life, fed by their mother's milk. After that they must learn to hunt fish for themselves. Grey seals can live for up to thirty years and are a protected species in Ireland.

Fun Facts

There are lots of Irish myths and legends around seals. Selkies were said to be half human, half seal. Some families in Connemara and Kerry were even said to have descended from seals!

Atlantic Puffins

They may look cute and cuddly, but these hardy birds are built to survive! They spend much of their lives at sea hunting fish so they need to be strong flyers and clever hunters.

In the summer they come ashore to nest and lay their eggs on cliffs and sea stacks. In Ireland they can be seen on the Cliffs of Moher in Clare and on Horn Head in Donegal. Plus of course Puffin Island near Skellig Michael in Kerry (and many other offshore islands).

Puffins sometimes take a year or two off having baby puffins. Scientists think this is due to stress – they need a break from looking after little pufflings! They mate for life, staying with the same partner and nesting in the same nest or 'burrow' every year.

Hoppy's Fun Facts

🐾 Baby puffins have the best name ever – pufflings!

🐾 Puffins make a funny growling noise that sounds like a lawnmower or a chainsaw. Strange but true!

🐾 During the filming of Star Wars on the Irish rocky island, Skellig Michael, there were so many puffins in their shots the film makers had two choices – digitally edit each bird out (a huge task) – or make them part of the Star Wars universe. So the Irish puffins became Star Wars porgs!

Fungie, Ireland's Famous Dolphin

Fungie is a male bottle-nosed dolphin who lives in the waters around Dingle in Co. Kerry. He was first spotted in 1984 by the lighthouse keeper. Although he is a wild dolphin he seems to enjoy human company, which is unusual. He has been entertaining and delighting locals and tourists for over thirty years. He enjoys swimming in the wake of fishing and tour boats.

In the wild dolphins can live up to fifty years and Fungie is a much loved older member of the Dingle community!

Jellyfish

Jellyfish are old, old animals. The oldest ancestors of modern day jellies lived at least 500 million years ago, and maybe as long as 700 million years ago. That makes jellyfish three-times as old as the first dinosaurs!

They have an opening or 'mouth' inside their body. They also use this mouth for getting rid of waste AND moving around.

They move by squirting water through their mouth which propels them forwards.

Jellyfish eat a variety of 'zooplankton' or tiny sea creatures.

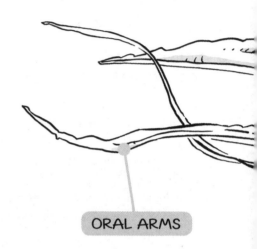

ORAL ARMS

Paws for Thought

An Irish woman called Maude Delap was known as the 'Jellyfish Lady'.

She started studying jellyfish as a teenager and was the first person in the world to successfully rear them in captivity. She kept them in huge glass jars, which she shot through with bubbles of oxygen (like a modern aquarium), and worked out exactly how to feed them.

Scientists had always been puzzled by the complex lifecycle of the jellyfish, but it was Maude who finally cracked it! She published her work in 1901 in 'The Irish Naturalist' journal. Scientists still use her research to this day.

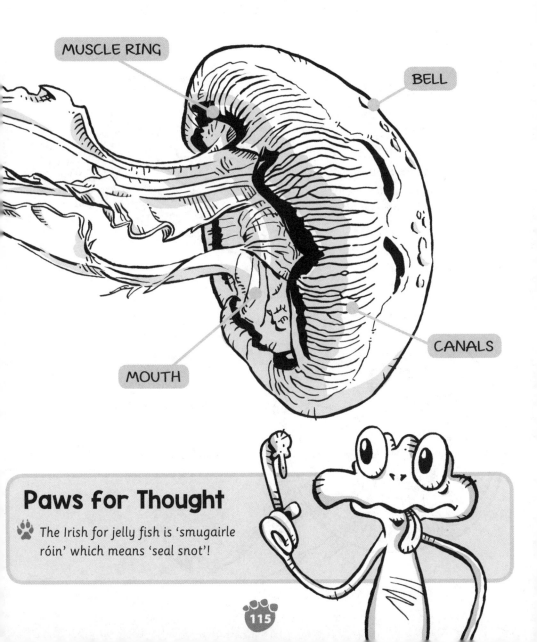

MUSCLE RING

BELL

CANALS

MOUTH

Paws for Thought

🐾 The Irish for jelly fish is 'smugairle róin' which means 'seal snot'!

There are five types of jellyfish native to Ireland:

Barrel

These are funny-looking fellows! They have a large dome shaped ghostly white body.

Instead of tentacles they have eight 'arms' dangling from the dome, each with a 'mouth' on the end – which look a bit like cauliflower florets.

No sting, but some people can be allergic to touching them

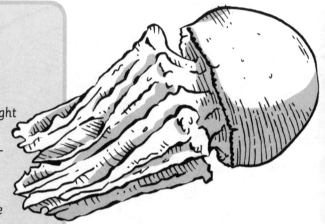

Common (or Moon)

It has a transparent or see-through body with four pinky-purple rings on its back.

No tentacles.

Very mild sting.

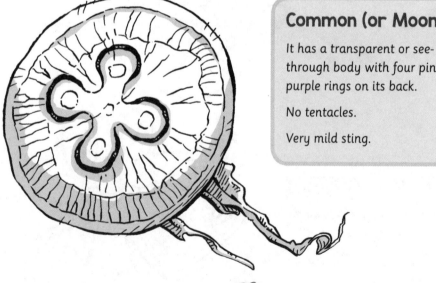

Compass

White jellyfish with reddish-brown v-shaped patterns on its back.

Long tentacles.

Painful sting – like a nettle sting.

Blue

These fellows have translucent body and blue rings inside – hence the name!

Lots of tentacles.

Painful sting.

Lion's Mane

Gives a nasty sting and can be dangerous if you are allergic to its venom.
You can see how it got its name – it looks like a lion's mane.

In the Forest and Countryside

Owls

Three kinds of owl live in Ireland – the long-eared owl, the barn owl and the short-eared owl.

Owls hunt at night and like eating insects, birds and small mammals like mice. They usually swallow their prey whole and after a few hours they cough up a pellet. This contains the bits of their food that they couldn't digest.

They have large eyes at the front of their heads. They can rotate their heads more than 270 degrees, which means they can almost see behind themselves! They have a strong, hooked bill and sharp claws that help them catch and crush their prey.

Long-eared owl

Owls have excellent hearing; they have one ear higher up than the other, which allows them to pinpoint the location of sounds, and the shape of their facial feathers channels sounds towards their ears. Their feathers are so soft they make almost no noise when they are flying. They make their nests in trees, in rock crevices or old buildings like castles or barns.

Barn owl

Short-eared owl

Hoppy's Feathery Facts

🐾 Little owls are called owlets.

🐾 The barn owl is the signature bird of RTE's 'The Late Late Show' and features in the opening sequence.

Badgers

There could be as many as 250,000 badgers living in Ireland. They like to live in woodlands or grasslands, but they are shy creatures who only come out at night, so they are hard to spot.

The badgers found in Ireland are called European badgers. They are about a metre long and can weigh up to 18kg. Male badgers are called boars, females are sows and young badgers are cubs.

Badgers have sharp teeth and eat small mammals like mice or rabbits, plus insects, birds and frogs.

YIKES!

They also eat nuts, fruit, roots and tubers (like potatoes). One of their very favourite things to eat are earthworms – they can eat up to two hundred of them in one night!

Badgers are brilliant at digging. They are one of the fastest animal diggers in the world. They have strong front paws that act like shovels and long sharp claws to cut through the dirt. They can also run fast over small distances – up to 30km/h!

Badgers live in tunnels and 'rooms' underground called 'setts'. Do you have your own bedroom? Badgers do! They are very civilized animals indeed!

They are clean creatures and like to do their poos and wees in a special pit they dig outside their setts. They won't eat inside their setts either and they change the grass they use as bedding on a regular basis.

Setts can have many different entrances so the badgers can come and go as they please. Some setts are used for many generations of badgers (who can live up to fifteen years). If there is a road near one of the entrances to a badger's sett, sadly the animals often get knocked down and killed.

Frogs

Three amphibians live in Ireland – the common frog, the natterjack toad and the smooth newt.

Amphibians are cold-blooded vertebrates (animals with backbones) that can live both in and out of the water. They are really old animals – frogs first appeared over 300 million years ago!

Finally – the best and most important animals in the whole entire universe – frogs of course!

Irish frogs can be lots of different colours, from green to brown or even yellow. They have markings on their skin to help camouflage them from predators like hedgehogs and herons. They can also change their skin colour to adapt to the environment they are in – this takes about two hours.

Irish frogs hibernate in winter to avoid the frosty weather. They curl away under stones or logs or even buried in the mud at the bottom of the pond, where they stay hidden, breathing through their skin.

Frogs have four fingers and five toes and are very strong swimmers and jumpers. They like to live near ponds, streams or bog pools.

They eat flies, slugs, spiders and insects. They have really long tongues which are handy for catching flies and insects. Frogs can live for up to ten years.

Frogs have a really interesting life cycle – I bet you know it! Their amazing transformation is called 'metamorphosis'.

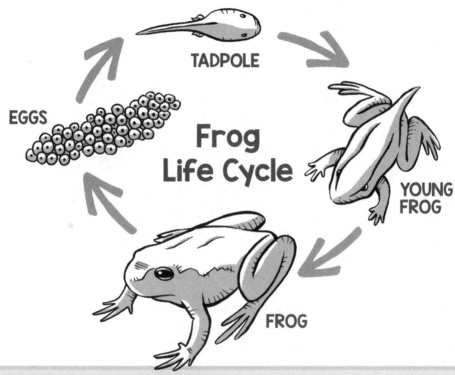

Hoppy's Fun Facts

🐾 Natterjack toads can't hop like frogs, they can only walk or run. They are only found in Kerry and Wexford and are very rare. They like to live near the sea in sandy or marshy areas.

🐾 Frogs, like snakes, shed their skin when it gets old. They pull it off using their feet and sometimes – look away if you are squeamish – they even eat it!

Weird and Wonderful Animals

Tardigrades

Tardigrades are also known as water bears or moss piglets. They were first discovered around 1773 by a German man called Johann August Ephraim Goeze. He called them 'Little Water Bears', because he thought they moved like funny little bears over moss or lichen, slow and lumbering!

There are land, marine and freshwater tardigrades. They are tiny creatures of only 0.5mm – three or four of them could happily fit end to end along the top of a pin – and they can be seen using a microscope. They have eight legs with tiny claws or suckers at the ends.

They have been found in different habitats all over the planet – from mud volcanoes, to the deepest oceans and the highest mountains. They can live in the north and south poles and in tropical rain forests – they thrive everywhere!

There are about 1,150 know species of tardigrades in the world. Most eat tiny pieces of plant matter or bacteria. What makes them truly remarkable is their ability to survive in the harshest conditions around. They can even survive outer space.

In 2007 dehydrated tardigrades were taken into space for ten days on the FOTON-M3 mission. On landing back on earth, two-thirds of them were successfully brought back to life. Tardigrades have survived several space missions since then.

Tardigrades can go without water and food for – this is truly mind-blowing – up to thirty years! They go into a special state of being called cryptobiosis, curling into a ball called a 'tun' and waiting until conditions are better for their survival. If they are reintroduced to water they can come to life again in a few hours. Magic!

Lampreys

Lampreys, sometimes called Lamprey Eels, are a very ancient kind of jawless fish. They have round mouths full of sharp, hooked teeth. To eat – if you are squeamish stop reading now – lampreys can stick onto the side of another fish, bore into their flesh and suck their blood!

They have long bodies and can grow up to a metre long. The ancient Romans loved eating lampreys and they were also very popular in the Middle Ages. They are still considered a delicacy in some parts of Europe such as Latvia. You can even buy pickled lamprey in the supermarkets in Finland!

HOLY MOLEY!

PART 5
WHERE IN THE WORLD?
Animal Habitats

What is a Habitat?

A habitat is the place where an animal lives. There are lots of different sorts of habitats. Animals live in the habitat that best suits their needs, a location that gives them water, food and somewhere safe to shelter.

A habitat, along with all its plants and animals, is called an ecosystem.

There are seven main habitats in the world:

I live in a tropical rainforest in Brazil, South America – that's my habitat.

Tropical Rainforests

Forests

Oceans

Or Hoppyville!

Deserts

Grasslands

Polar Ice

Mountains

Over the next few pages we will meet the animals that live in some of these habitats.

Adaptations

Over time, some animals 'adapt' to suit their habitat – this means they change so they can live and thrive in their chosen habitat.

> My webbed feet help me swim and the sticky pads on my toes help me grip tree branches.

> My sticky tongue and wide mouth help me catch flies and insects

Remember that clever scientist Charles Darwin who studied animals and evolution in the 19th century? He discovered that over time animals' bodies and behaviour could adapt or change to help them find food.

Sometimes a change was really useful to the animal and it was passed on to its children. He called this 'natural selection'. It is sometimes called 'survival of the fittest'.

Here's how natural selection works:

The giraffe with the highest neck – let's call her Lofty – reaches the highest leaves on the trees and eats the most.

So Lofty survives when there is not so much food around. The giraffes with shorter necks do not survive and eventually die out.

Lofty goes on to produce babies with long necks, who can also reach the tippy-top leaves.

Animal Adaptors

Polar bears have adapted to live on ice and to hunt in water. The bottoms of their feet are covered in thick black pads, which have soft bumps called 'papillae' to help them grip the ice.

My friend, Ariel the Wallace's flying frog has big webbed hands and feet and special 'flying' skin that stretches between her limbs. This helps her glide through the forest, from tree to tree. Amazing!

Woodpeckers have strong beaks and a hard skull. Perfect for pecking and hammering tree bark to find insects underneath. They can also carve out holes in tree trunks to make a warm, safe place for their nests. Clever birds!

Hoppy's Froggy Facts

👣 Wallace's flying frog is named after Alfred Russel Wallace, who thought of the theory of natural selection at the same time as Charles Darwin.

Some animals are so highly adapted that they can only live in one habitat – like the giant panda who only eats bamboo. They can only live wild in the mountains of China where there are still some bamboo forests to feed on. This is why it's so important to protect habitats all over the world.

About Hoppy's Home:
The Tropical Rainforests

Hi, everyone!

Finally we come to my home, Hoppyville!

I live in the Amazon rainforest in Brazil, South America. The Amazon rainforest is 5.5 million km squared – that's big! It's also half of the world's rainforest so it's a really important habitat. Scientists think there could be as many as 400 billion trees in the Amazon.

Tropical rainforests are also found in Africa, Southeast Asia and Madagascar. They are located around the equator thanks to all the rain, and though they only account for 6% of the world's surface area, rainforests contain more than half the planet's animal and plant species. A single tropical rainforest can be home to more than a thousand species – more different species are found here than in any other habitat in the world – this makes them pretty special places.

Tropical rainforests have many different layers that are home to different kinds of animals.

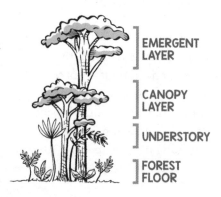

EMERGENT LAYER

CANOPY LAYER

UNDERSTORY

FOREST FLOOR

Emergent Layer

At the very top level there are giant trees called emergent trees or 'emergents' that poke through the canopy into the light.

These trees must cope with high temperatures from the blazing sun.

(Silvery gibbons and howler monkeys live here.)

Canopy Layer

This layer is very thick and only 2 to 15 per cent of sunlight passes through it. It forms a roof over the rainforest and gives both shelter and food to lots of the rainforest's animals.

Most rainforest animals – monkeys, birds, insects, snakes, bats – live in the canopy. (Orangutans and hornbills live here.)

Understory

I live in the understory – the layer between the canopy and the forest floor – which has smaller trees and plants like palms and ferns. Other animals that live in the understory include the slow loris and the leopard.

Forest Floor

And finally the forest floor. It can be pretty gloomy down there as most of the light is blocked out by the trees. It teems with insect life – be careful if you're ever walking in a rainforest, the insects can grow pretty big. Strong boots or shoes are needed!

(Rhinoceros beetles and rainforest pigs like peccaries live here.)

What's the Difference Between a Rainforest and a Jungle?

A rainforest is dense forest. Little sunlight reaches the ground to allow plants to grow so it is easy to walk around.

Jungles are often found in rainforests – near rivers or where the light can get through to allow plants to thrive. Jungles have thick plants near the ground that can be almost impossible to walk through.

In the olden days rainforests were often explored from the river – by boat. The explorers didn't venture far past the river so they thought the rainforest was all jungle-like! Old books and films like the 'Tarzan' series by Edgar Rice Burroughs and The Jungle Book by Rudyard Kipling were often set in 'the jungle'.

Some Other Animals of the Tropical Rainforest

Tippy Toppers of the Emergent Trees - Howler Monkeys

The howler monkey's incredibly loud, raspy call can be heard over 5km away and they use it to call out to each other and to defend their territory. They are the loudest land animal on the planet. The noise is so loud early 'jungle' explorers thought there were monsters in the trees!

The male howler monkeys have an enlarged bone in their throats (the hyoid bone), which makes their calls so loud.

They eat mostly flowers, leaves, bark, fruit and moss.

Canopy - Toucan

Toucans are famous for their large, colourful yellow and orange beaks. The toucan has the longest beak of any bird in the world in relation to its body size. (The Australian pelican holds the record for the longest beak of all birds).

Toucans eat mostly fruit. This makes them 'frugivores' (fruit eaters).Their long beaks allow them to reach fruits dangling from branches.

They live in small flocks and communicate with each other using a croaky call. It sounds almost like a frog call!

Understory - Leopard

Leopards have adapted to live in lots of different habitats, from deserts to rainforests. What they eat depends on their habitat – rainforest leopards eat birds, small mammals and monkeys.

They hunt at night and then drag their prey into a tree so they can eat undisturbed. They can lift animals three times their own body weight using their powerful jaws.

Forest Floor - Leafcutter Ant

Leafcutter ants are known for their amazing ability to carry leaves that are up to fifty times their own body weight. They are hard and fast workers and can strip a tree of all its leaves in less than a day.

They don't eat the leaves they carry. They put them in a special chamber in their colony's nest. A leaf fungus grows on these leaves and this is the ants' food – it's like an underground fungus farm. Clever ants!

Up to ten million ants can live in one of their colonies. That's a whole lot of ants!

All About Me!

The most important animal in the rainforest (and in the world, naturally!) – ME!

Red-Eyed Tree Frog

It's nice and damp in the rainforest from all the rain, so we don't need to be near a stream or pond to keep our skin moist.

We move around in the trees using the suckers on our toes to grip the leaves and branches.

We find delicious insects to eat and shoot out our long sticky tongues to catch them.

We keep our eyes tight shut when we are hiding. But if an animal threatens us we open our eyes and give them a scary bright-red glare!

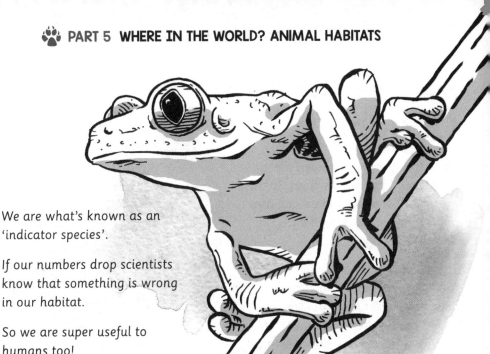

We are what's known as an 'indicator species'.

If our numbers drop scientists know that something is wrong in our habitat.

So we are super useful to humans too!

Hoppy's Amazing Tropical Rainforest Animal Facts

🐾 The electric blue wings of the blue morpho butterfly are so bright that pilots can spot them when they are flying over the Amazon. It is one of the biggest butterflies in the world – its wings can be as large as 20cm across.

🐾 The aye-aye is a small lemur, so rare that for many years scientists thought it was extinct. It lives in the rainforests of Madagascar and only comes out at night.

Keep on Swimming:
Oceans

Earth is not called the Blue Planet for nothing! The oceans cover 70 per cent of our planet's surface and are home to a huge variety of different animals.

The five ocean regions – the Atlantic, the Arctic, the Indian, Pacific and Southern oceans make up around 97 per cent of the world's water. All these oceans together are called the World Ocean.

There are lots of different kinds of marine habitats – from coral reefs, to rocky shores and deep ocean trenches like the Marianas Trench in the Pacific, the deepest known trench in the world's oceans. It is thought to be over 11km deep.

Life began in the oceans over 3.5 billion years ago and they are still teeming with life to this day. Scientists know there are over 230,000 different species of animals in the ocean. But there may be millions more, just waiting to be discovered!

Sunlight Zone
Sharks, fish, jellyfish

Twilight Zone
Whales, squid, turtles

Midnight Zone
Lobsters and crabs

The Abyss
Deep sea creatures

Trench

Ahhh – now I sea...

Hoppy's Amazing Animal Facts

Did you know that corals are colonies of tiny animals that are related to jellyfish? Fish love to live in the nooks and crannies of coral reefs, like the clown fish, made famous by the movie, Finding Nemo.

It is hard to hide in the ocean so fish swim together in groups called schools to stay safe. When they all swim together it's hard for a predator to pick off one fish to eat! Clever fish!

Animals of the Ocean

The Great White Shark

Of all the creatures in the sea the one that makes most
people shiver is the great white shark!

They can grow to over six metres (longer than a car!)
and live as long as seventy years. They eat anything
they can get their teeth on, from seals to fish. And they
have a lot of teeth! Over three hundred triangular teeth as sharp as daggers, arranged in
rows. But whatever the myths, fewer than ten people a year are killed by sharks.

The good news is that the waters around Ireland are too cold for great white sharks.
They are mainly found around the United States, South Africa, Japan, Chile, and the
Mediterranean.

Giant Squid

Giant squid are among of the most
mysterious animals on the planet
– they have very rarely been
seen by humans. At a whopping 13m long or even more, they are enormous! How can
something so huge remain hidden? Well, they live in deep, deep water. It wasn't until 2006
that scientists managed to video a giant squid in its natural habitat.

The giant squid also has the largest eyes on earth – up to 30cm across – that's a whole lot
of eyeball! They eat small fish, other squid and crabs. They catch food with their feeding
tentacles and crush it in their sharp beak before swallowing it.

Giant squid are known to live in the North Atlantic, the North Pacific and in the waters
around New Zealand and South Africa. Scientists think there are lots more amazing deep
water creatures in our oceans just waiting to be discovered!

By-the-Wind Sailor or Velella

What a cool name this jellyfish has – By-the-Wind Sailor. This small electric-blue jellyfish is called this because it has a sail on its back that helps it sail along with the wind, like a little boat.

It has tentacles that hang in the water to catch plankton to eat. But don't worry, its sting is harmless to humans unless you are allergic to it.

By-the-Wind Sailors can sometimes be seen in Irish waters – keep your eyes peeled in the summer for these tiny treasures of the sea!

The Japanese Spider Crab

Japanese spider crabs are huge! Their legs can span five metres from claw to claw. They can survive when they lose up to three legs and sometimes their legs grow back.

They live in deep water around Japan and are the world's largest crab. The Japanese call them 'Taka-ashi-gani' or 'tall legs crab'.

They may look scary, but they are said to be gentle creatures. I still wouldn't like to meet one if I was swimming in the ocean!

Hot, Hot, Hot:
Deserts

The hottest desert on earth is the Sahara Desert in Africa. It can reach temperatures of up to 48C in the summer during the day and it only rains once or twice a year. It's huge – almost the size of the entire United States of America – over 9 million kilometres squared.

You have to be a pretty tough cookie to live in the Sahara, but remember our old friend Darwin and his evolution and natural selection? Desert animals have adapted brilliantly to survive the harsh conditions.

Adaptations for the desert include:

Size

Desert animals are often small – so they need less food and water to survive

Burrowing

Many animals like the desert jerboa (a rodent) spend the hottest part of the day underground in burrows. They come out at night to look for food and water when it's cooler.

Pale coats

Animals like the fennec fox have pale coats to reflect the sun, keep them cool and hide them from animals they are trying to track or hunt.

Big hooves or feet

Some animals – like the addax or screwhorn antelope – have adapted to have big feet to help them walk on the sand. It spreads their weight out and stops them sinking into the sand when they walk.

Hoppy's Fun Facts

 Sometimes there is an oasis or 'wadi' in the desert, water left over from ancient lakes or where a spring reaches the surface. Special desert plants and trees grow around the oasis, like tree ferns and palm trees. There can even be crocodiles in an oasis!

Sand dunes sometimes have avalanches (like snowy mountains), sending piles of sand down their slopes. This creates a loud hum that can be heard over 6km away!

Animals of the Desert

Arabian Camel (or Dromedary)

Arabian camels are sometimes called 'ships of the desert' as they transport people and goods across the desert. They can go for days without water. When they do find it they can drink a huge thirty litres in minutes. Wild Bactrian camels are adapted to be able to drink even salty water safely.

Arabian camels have one hump, long narrow nostrils, which they can close, and thick eyelashes that help protect them from sandstorms.
If sand gets stuck in their eyes, they can blink it away using a third transparent eyelid.

Their large, wide hooves with two toes help stop them sinking into the sand. Their thick, leathery lips help them eat tough plants and even spiny and thorny ones. There are about 35 million camels in the world, of which 95 per cent are Arabian camels.

The other type of camel is called the Bactrian camel. They have two humps and are found mainly in Central Asia.

The nomads (travelling people) of the Gobi desert in Asia rely on Bactrian camels for their milk, meat and wool. There are small numbers of wild Bactrian camels, approx 600 in China and 350 in Mongolia.

Hoppy's Fun Facts

Many people think that camels store water in their humps, but that's not true – they actually store fat. This means they can go without eating for a long time. Also, storing all their fat in one place minimises their insulation and keeps them cool. The hump gets smaller and smaller as the fat is used up.

African Dung Beetles

African dung beetles rely on dung or poo to survive. As soon as they smell a fresh pile of dung they rush towards it and form a dung ball. They then push this dung ball to a safe place and bury it. The dung ball can be over fifty times the weight of the beetle and it can still push it. Once it's buried, they eat the dung.

There are different kinds of dung beetles – 'rollers' who roll the dung (like the African dung beetle), 'tunnellers' who make holes to bury the dung, and 'dwellers' who live in the dung itself.

Why would any animal want to eat poo?

Good question! When an animal eats some of the food is undigested – or not absorbed by the body – and remains in the poo. It's actually the liquid in the dung that adult dung beetles suck up using special mouth parts.

They also lay eggs in the dung. When their larvae (baby dung beetles) hatch, they are surrounded by lovely, smelly dung to eat!

By burying and then eating the dung, they improve the soil and also spread plants' seeds over the desert.

Hoppy's Fun Facts

Scientists have proved that African dung beetles use the stars to navigate – strange but true! At night they climb on top of their ball of dung and find their way around using the stars to guide them. They are the only invertebrate know to navigate by the stars!

The Ancient Egyptians believed that dung beetles or 'scarabs' were sacred. The little beetle rolling his ball of dung across the ground reminded them of their god Khepri, who rolled the sun across the sky every morning.

Images of scarabs are found in Ancient Egyptian art.

When people died in Ancient Egypt, scarabs were carved out of green precious stone and placed on the dead person's chest before they were buried. This was called a 'heart scarab' and it was said to help the dead person's journey into the afterlife.

Roaming Free:
Grasslands

The Beautiful African Savanna

Grasslands form in areas where it's too dry for many trees and forests and too wet to be a desert. So it's somewhere in between!

The main plants growing here are – the clue is in the name – grasses! They have big root systems below the ground and are very hardy. If the grass leaves are eaten or cut away or damaged by fire or drought, they re-grow from the base of the plant.

There are two main types of grasslands: tropical savannas, like the African savanna, and temperate grasslands, like the American prairies or the pampas of South America.

The African savanna covers about half of the African continent.

Big cats like lions and cheetahs live on the African savanna, hunting animals like zebra and antelope. The Serengeti region of the African savanna is home to over 1.7 million wildebeests, 500,000 gazelles, 250,000 zebra and 3,000 lions. The animals' poo helps to fertilize the soil, which makes more grass grow.

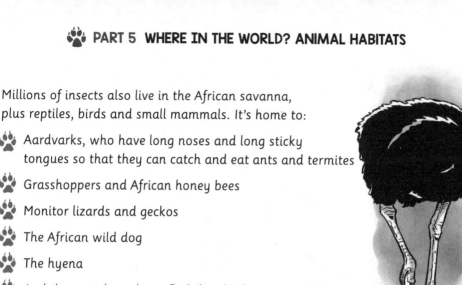

Millions of insects also live in the African savanna, plus reptiles, birds and small mammals. It's home to:

🐾 Aardvarks, who have long noses and long sticky tongues so that they can catch and eat ants and termites

🐾 Grasshoppers and African honey bees

🐾 Monitor lizards and geckos

🐾 The African wild dog

🐾 The hyena

🐾 And the ostrich – a large flightless bird

Hoppy's Fun Facts

🐾 Scavengers like jackals and vultures feast on the remains of animals killed and left behind by the big cats. These remains are known as 'carrion'. Scavengers are useful animals as they keep the grasslands clean of rotting meat.

If you're squeamish, stop reading now!

Some scavengers take their job very seriously. African white-backed vultures poke their heads inside an animal carcass to get at all the meat. They have long, strong necks – with no feathers on them to get dirty -- to help them do this.

EWW!

Animals of the Grasslands

Lions

Lions are what's called 'apex predators'. This means they are at the top of the food chain and have no natural predators.

They are natural hunters and are very good at their job! No wonder they are known as the 'King of the Beasts' and feature in all kinds of books and movies, from The Lion, the Witch and the Wardrobe by CS Lewis to The Lion King.

There are two subspecies of lions – the African lion and the Asiatic lion.

Sadly the Asiatic lion is endangered, there are only about 600 of them surviving – all living in the Gir National Park in India.

Around 10,000 years ago lions roamed Europe, Asia and America. Now they are found mainly in Africa. There are now less than 20,000 lions left in the wild. And sadly humans are to blame. They have been hunted by humans for sport and killed by farmers for hundreds of years.

Lions are very sociable animals and love company. They live in groups called prides.

Male lions have shaggy manes. Their job is to protect the pride and guard its territory. Female lions do most of the hunting. A male lion's roar is very loud, it can be heard over 8km away.

Lions mostly hunt at night and rest during the day. They will eat any animal they can kill, from zebra to antelope. On average they eat 8-9kg of meat a day – that's around twenty-five human meals!

Hoppy's Fun Facts

 Big cats – like lions – pull in their claws when they walk or run, unlike dogs who leave their claws out. This makes it easy to tell their tracks apart.

LION PAW PRINT

HYENA PAW PRINT

Elephants

Elephants are the largest land animal on the planet. There are three different species of elephant – the African forest elephant, the African bush elephant and the Asian elephant, which is smaller and found in India and Southeast Asia.

Elephants eat grasses and leaves. They drink by using their long trunks to suck up water and squirt it into their mouths. They can drink up to 300 litres of water a day and also squirt water over their backs to keep them cool in the sun.

Female elephants mostly live in herds of eight to thirteen adult female family members and their children. The herd is headed up a senior female elephant called the matriarch.

Male elephants either live alone or in all male bachelor herds.

African bush elephants' huge ears look just like the shape of the African continent – strange but true!

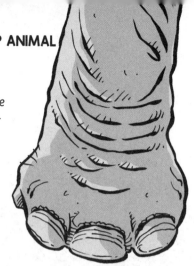

Elephants walk on their toes, with their heels off the ground. They have a huge pad of fatty tissue under their foot bones which helps absorb their huge weight and means they can move around comfortably and quietly.

It would be like a human wearing a pair of runners with big, soft spongy soles!

Hoppy's Fun Facts

🐾 Asian elephants have one piece of pointed skin called a finger on their trunk.

African elephants have two.

These fingers are very sensitive, like human finger tips.

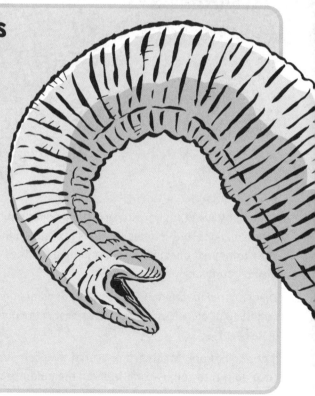

Armadillos

Armadillos live in rainforests, grasslands amd semi-deserts of South and Central America, along with pumas, pampas fox and guanaco (wild llama). Armadillo means 'little armoured one' in Spanish and they are the only living mammal with a hard shell or 'carapace'.

There are many different species of armadillo – the smallest is the pink fairy armadillo at only 15cm long. The largest is the giant armadillo, which is the size of a sheep!

If armadillos are threatened or scared they can jump up to 1m in the air. They do this to confuse and frighten the predator who often runs away.

Their shells are made up of around 2,000 scales called 'scutes'. They mainly eat birds' eggs, small animals and beetles. They feed at night and rest in their burrows during the day.

Hoppy's Fun Facts

🐾 The modern armadillo is related to the ancient and now extinct glyptodon, which was a huge, heavily armoured mammal that lived around 2 to 10 million years ago.

They lived in South America and were the size and weight of a small car!

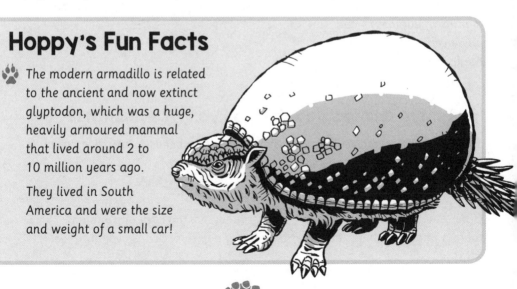

Ice, Ice, Baby:
Polar Ice

The coldest habitats on the planets are near the North Pole and the South Pole.

Most animals that live on ice and snow are warm-blooded, although a few cold-blooded animals have adapted to survive in the icy conditions.

Conditions are harsh – sub-zero temperatures, hurricane force winds, months of darkness – and animals need to be very hardy to live here.

How have animals adapted to live in icy habitats?

Some like whales and seals grow a thick layer of fat beneath their skin called blubber. This keeps them insulated from the cold.

Polar bears grow thick, dense fur to keep them warm.

Other animals, like lemmings, go underground, making cosy burrows and tunnels under the snow. In winter they rarely pop their heads over ground!

Arctic and Antarctic

Hello from the Antarctic!

The Arctic to the far north of planet earth is made up of frozen ocean, surrounded by cold, wild land known as tundra.

It's slightly warmer than the Antarctic, but its winters still reach a freezing -40 C during the winter.

The Antarctic or Antarctica lies to the far south of planet earth and is made up of ice up to 5km thick. The average yearly temperature is -49 C and it's dark all the time in the winter.

It's super windy in the Antarctic, with wind speeds of over 300km per hour. Almost all life here lives in or by the sea.

I'm freezing!

Me too!

Animals of the Arctic

Polar Bears

Do polar bears eat penguins? No – because polar bears live in the Arctic and penguins live in the Antarctic!

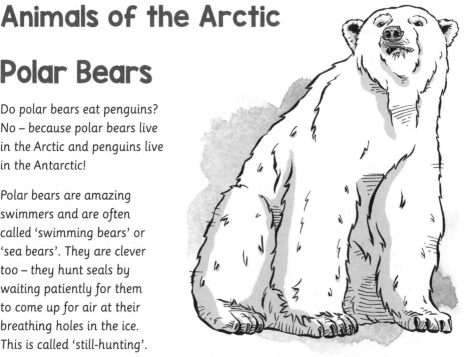

Polar bears are amazing swimmers and are often called 'swimming bears' or 'sea bears'. They are clever too – they hunt seals by waiting patiently for them to come up for air at their breathing holes in the ice. This is called 'still-hunting'. Sometimes they wait for three or four hours – that's a long time to wait for your dinner!

Although polar bears look white, their fur is actually transparent; the strands are hollow and reflect the light. Underneath their skin is black! This helps them soak up rays from the sun and stay warm. They have amazing noses and can smell seals from around a kilometre away.

The mother bear gives birth and looks after her cubs in a breeding den that she cuts out of a snowdrift. As the cubs grow, she digs tunnels and chambers for them to live and play in. Global warming means that polar bears are struggling to find snow drifts big enough to create their dens in.

Polar bears used to be hunted for their fur and meat, but now the biggest threat to them is climate change.

Reindeer

Most of us know reindeer as the clever animals who pull Santa's sleigh at Christmas! However they are very important to the people of the Arctic.

In North America reindeer are called 'caribou' and the Inuit call them 'tuktu'.

Reindeer eat grasses, ferns, leaves from trees and bushes and also mosses and lichen.

They are known for their large antlers, which are covered in a furry velvet when they are growing. No set of antlers are alike – they are like human fingerprints! Both male and female reindeer can grow antlers.

In many countries people eat reindeer meat and it's often made into sausages or meatballs. Cheese and yoghurt can be made from reindeer milk.

In the wild, some reindeer make long migrations of up to 3,000km a year to find food. They move in vast herds of over a thousand animals.

Animals of the Antarctic

Penguins

There are lots of different kinds of penguins in the Antarctic. They eat fish, squid and krill and have adapted to become brilliant swimmers. Instead of using their wings to fly, they use them to power through the water like flippers. They have no predators on land (no polar bears, remember?), so they don't need to be able to fly away.

They live in colonies of up to 60,000 birds and huddle together to keep warm.

Male Emperor penguins are famous for looking after the eggs while the mothers go hunting for two months. They balance their egg on their feet, tucked into a special pouch called a brood pouch, which keeps the egg warm.

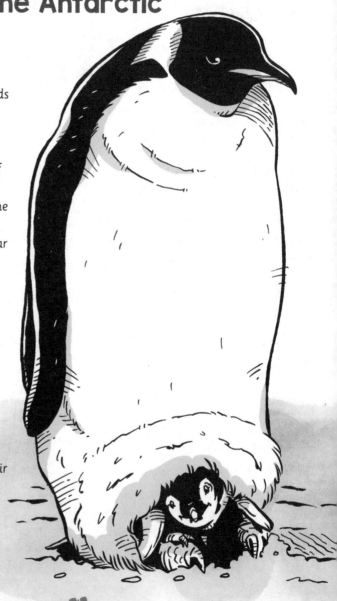

Antarctic Krill

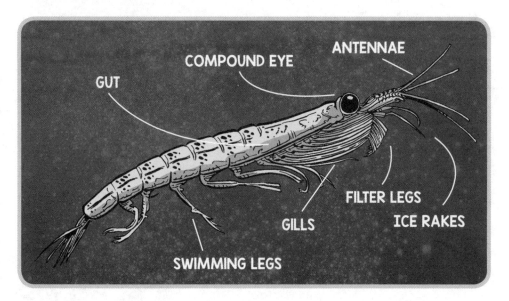

ANTENNAE

COMPOUND EYE

GUT

GILLS

FILTER LEGS

ICE RAKES

SWIMMING LEGS

Without this tiny pink animal, most of the other animals of the Antarctic could not exist! Krill are tiny crustaceans no bigger than your little finger that are eaten by whales, seals, penguins, squid and fish.

Every day they drift up from the deep to the water's surface – this is called vertical migration.

These little creatures can live for up to ten years – that's no mean feat for a creature with so many predators!

Adéline penguins eat so many krill that their poo (guano) is pink and often stains their feathers.

You could try krill yourself! In Japan if you see 'okiami' on a menu, that is krill! And in the Philippines krill are used to make a salty paste called 'bagoong'!

Higher and Higher:
Mountains

Almost 25 per cent of the planet's surface is made up of mountains. Up high the conditions can be harsh –

Yodel-eh-eee-hoo!

 Low temperatures

 Less oxygen in the air

 Barren land with very few plants to eat

 Strong winds

But many animals have adapted to thrive in these difficult conditions.

The highest mountain range on earth is the Himalayas. Mount Everest, the highest mountain peak in the world is in the Himalayas.

Snow Leopards

The snow leopard is an endangered animal that lives in the mountains of Central Asia. There are only around 5,000 left in the world. They have thick fur, which helps keep them warm in the cold, and wide, fur-covered feet that help them to walk on the snow.

Snow leopards eat mountain goats, sheep, rabbits and other small animals. They are known as 'Ghosts of the Mountain' as they are hard to spot. Sometimes their paw prints in the snow are the only clue as to where they are. They do not roar, but do make growling and hissing noises.

In the fantasy series, His Dark Materials by Philip Pullman, Lord Asriel's dæmon is a snow leopard named Stelmaria.

Golden Eagles

Golden Eagles are found in mountainous areas of Europe, North America, North Africa and Asia. They are famous for their fancy air shows or 'sky dances', swooping and soaring to attract a mate or mark a territory. They can reach speeds of 240km per hour when free-falling from the sky.

They build nests in cliffs and other high places. For such a large bird they have a very high-pitched, chirpy call – it sounds like a puppy yelping!

They are brilliant hunters and eat hares, rabbits, mice and birds. They swoop down on their prey and whip them up with their strong, sharp talons.

They are being reintroduced into the wild in Ireland. Watch out for them in the Glenveagh National Park in Co. Donegal.

Weird and Wonderful Animals

Immortal Jellyfish

The immortal jellyfish is found in the Mediterranean Sea and in the seas around Japan. It's a small, bell-shaped transparent jellyfish with a bright red stomach.

It is one of the only animals in the world who can go backwards – from adulthood to childhood! When an immortal jellyfish runs out of food, or has been attacked, instead of dying it can change back to it's baby stage – the polyp stage of life. This polyp is genetically identical to the original jellyfish, it just looks different.

And it can keep doing this – changing from its adult form back to its polyp form – whenever it needs to. So it lives on – forever – which is how it got its name.

However it can of course still be eaten by a shark or a sea turtle!

African Shoebills

Also called whale-headed storks, African shoebills are large birds of over 100cm tall. They got their name because their bill looks like a Dutch clog!

Chinese Water Deer

I'm not sure I'd want to meet a Chinese water deer in a dark forest! With their 5cm long tusks, they look like vampire deer, but they are shy animals who run away from danger.

They originally come from China, but there are some wild herds in England and France. They were accidentally released into the wild by private zoos.

Humpback Angler Fish

The humpback angler fish is a deep-water fish that has its own built-in light to lure prey towards it. The light is actually a lumpy piece of flesh (called an 'esca') that sticks out from the fish's forehead on a modified fin. The end of the esca is lit by bioluminescence – a chemical reaction produced by the fish. Fireflies also use bioluminescence to light up the sky.

What a clever fish!

 **PART 6**

PLEASE TAKE CARE OF US
Rare and Endangered Animals

Animals can be made extinct or wiped out for many reasons:

Climate change (which can also bring changes in the temperature of the sea).

Destruction or pollution of their habitat. If an animal's habitat is destroyed, they cannot survive.

Unfortunately, humans are to blame for cutting down forests, over-hunting or over-fishing, polluting oceans, seas and lakes. They are also responsible for poaching, which is the illegal hunting or capturing of wild animals.

Animals that are now extinct include:

The Dodo

The dodo was a flightless bird that lived in Mauritius, which was hunted into extinction by sailors. The last dodo was spotted in 1662.

There is a model of a dodo in the Natural History Museum in Dublin.

The Baiji

Also known as the Chinese river dolphin, this beautiful sea mammal lived in the Yangtze River for millions of years. Fishermen called the baijis 'Goddesses of the River' as they were said to bring good luck.

Although not officially listed as extinct, no one has seen a baiji since around 2002. It is thought that the pollution in the river is mostly to blame.

The Passenger Pigeon

Also known as the wild pigeon, there were millions of these birds alive at the beginning of the 19th century. In 1914 the very last one died in Cincinnati Zoo in America. The forests where they used to live were cut down for farmland, and also lots of people ate pigeon meat as it was cheap. So the poor passenger pigeon was finally hunted into extinction.

Paws for Thought: An Extinct Irish Animal

The giant Irish deer was a huge deer that lived around 7,000 years ago in Ireland. It stood over two metres tall and had huge antlers spanning nearly three metres!

Scientists are not sure why it became extinct – did its habitat change, was there a deadly deer disease that wiped it out or was it over-hunted by humans? Perhaps if you become a scientist in the future you will find out.

There are some giant Irish deer skeletons in the Natural History Museum in Dublin and fossils in the National Museum of Ireland.

Other Extinct Animals:

Steller's Sea Cow
EXTINCT AROUND 1770

Great Auk
EXTINCT AROUND 1850

Tasmanian Tiger
EXTINCT AROUND 1830

You can see some extinct animals, including the great auk, in the Zoological Museum in Trinity College Dublin which is open to the public during the summer. https://www.tcd.ie/Zoology/museum/

Animals at Risk

Blue Whales

Blue whales are the largest animals that have ever lived on earth (that we know of!). But they are now endangered. We think there are between 10,000 and 25,000 of them in our oceans today, which sounds a lot, but it's only the population of one large town like Carlow.

What happen? Whaling! By 1900 blue whales were nearly extinct due to whalers and their harpoon cannons. They were caught for their meat and their oil.

Blue whale populations are now slowly growing, but humans need to protect these amazing animals and make sure they are never hunted again.

Polar Bears

Polar bears live in the icy regions of Russia, Alaska, Norway, Canada and Greenland. There are 20,000 to 30,000 of them alive today, but their habitat is in danger.

They eat mainly seals, hunting them from floating pack ice. At present their ice is melting earlier and freezing later, leaving them less time to hunt seals.

Climate change – which is causing this – is having a drastic effect on polar bears.

Sunda Pangolin

Pangolins are amazing-looking animals – they have scales all over their bodies. They are sometimes described as a 'walking pine cone'!

They eat ants and termites and live in rainforests, mainly in Asia.

Sadly for pangolins their scales are used in traditional Chinese medicine. And now because they have been hunted and hunted there are very few of them left in the world and they are critically endangered. To find out more about how you can help protect these remarkable animals check out www.savepangolins.org

Other Animals at Risk Around the World

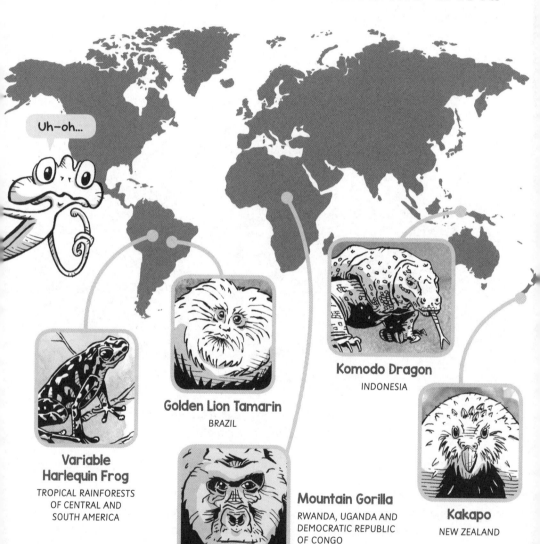

Uh-oh...

Komodo Dragon
INDONESIA

Golden Lion Tamarin
BRAZIL

**Variable
Harlequin Frog**
TROPICAL RAINFORESTS
OF CENTRAL AND
SOUTH AMERICA

Mountain Gorilla
RWANDA, UGANDA AND
DEMOCRATIC REPUBLIC
OF CONGO

Kakapo
NEW ZEALAND

Animals at Risk in Ireland

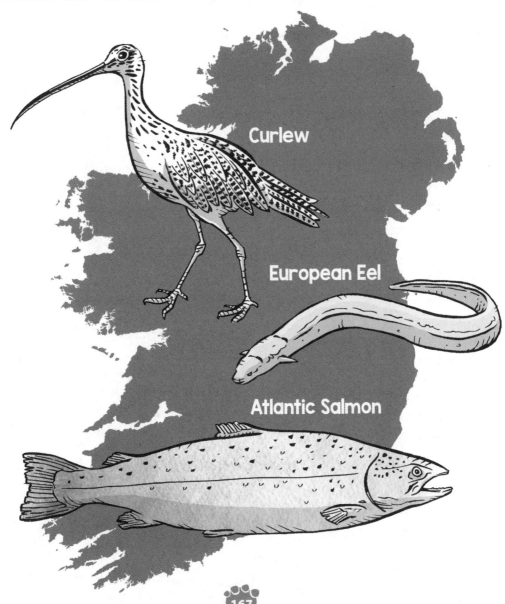

Curlew

European Eel

Atlantic Salmon

What's Going Wrong?

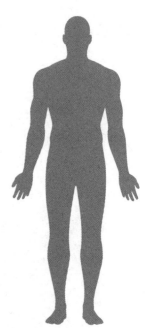

The International Union for the Conservation of Nature lists 112,432 species on earth, of which 30,178 species are threatened with extinction.

There is one animal that has changed the planet more than any other animal.

Can you guess which animal?

Yes, homo sapiens or humans.

Around 10,000 years ago humans were hunter/gatherers – they roamed around collecting just enough food to live.

Now the planet must support over 7 billion humans.

The Main Threats to our Planet's Animals:

Climate Change

Girls and boys all over Ireland and the world have been leading the way when it comes to climate change protests. They are trying to make the governments act before it's too late for all animals – including humans.

Global warming is leading to:

🐾 The extinction of animals

🐾 Melting of the polar ice caps

🐾 A rise in sea levels – for the last twenty years the sea levels have been rising about 3mm a year. This can cause flooding and erosion (eating away of the land by the sea).

🐾 A change in the acidity of the ocean. Extra carbon dioxide in the ocean over the last 200 years has made the acidity level rise by 30 per cent. Many marine animals, like coral reefs cannot survive this.

🐾 Extreme weather – like hurricanes, rainstorms and forest fires.

Loss of Habitat

Habitat loss is currently a threat to 85 per cent of all animal species. Forests are being cut down and humans are polluting the planet's ecosystems.

Over Hunting, Over Harvesting and Over Fishing

Humans need farming and fishing to survive. But we need to make sure we are not putting too much stress on the planet.

Fish are taken from the sea that humans don't even eat – this is called 'bycatch'. Big industrial nets are sweeping up fish before they have a chance to breed.

Dolphins in Danger

Up to a thousand cetaceans die every day in fishing nets. You can help them by looking for 'dolphin-friendly' symbols on your tins of tuna. These fishermen use fishing methods that are safer for whales and dolphins.

How You Can Help
Share What You Know

Tell people what you know or have learned from reading Animal Crackers about animals and what they need to survive.

Tell them that we frogs are in danger because our habitats are being destroyed.

Tell them that new species are appearing that eat us. The Louisiana crawfish (from America) was put into rivers in Europe. But here's the thing – it eats the larvae of European frogs and as they have never met a crawfish before they don't know to hide or to swim away, fast!

Tell them our skin is very thin so we are in real trouble when water is polluted – as it seeps into our bodies. My friend the golden toad from Costa Rica is now extinct and lots of my other friends are in danger of becoming extinct too.

If you make a pond in your back garden – even a small one – it will give us somewhere safe to live.

Reduce Your Carbon Footprint

Try to encourage your family to walk or cycle instead of jumping in the car.

Use a refillable water bottle in school and for sport.

Recycle things and fix things instead of throwing them away.

Use Your Voice

Ask your local politicians to help protect the planet and all its animals. No matter what age you are, you are an important member of the community. Make your voice heard!

Join the Green Schools committee in your school. If you don't have one, set one up.

Paws for Thought

Animals at Risk in Ireland: Bumblebees

🐾 There are 101 bee species in Ireland. twenty-one of these species are bumblebees.

The best-known bee is the honey bee; there are over 3,700 beekeepers on the island of Ireland keeping honeybees.

Honeybees beat their wings over 240 times a second to keep their bodies in the air.

There is a species of bumblebee that is only found on the Aran Islands – nowhere else In the world!

Scientists are worried that due to many factors like fewer wild areas where bees can find flowers and nectar and pesticides that a third of Ireland's bee species will be gone by 2030.

How You Can Help Bumblebees

The good news is that everyone can help by having an area in their gardens with wild flowers where the bees can find nectar.

As the great naturalist and conservationist Dr Jane Goodall once said:
'Surely, we do not want to live in a world without the great apes, our closest living relatives in the animal kingdom? A world where we can no longer marvel at the magnificent flight of bald eagles or hear the howl of wolves under the moon? A world not enhanced by the sight of a grizzly bear and her cubs hunting for berries in the wilderness?'

We want to live in a world full of amazing, remarkable animals! Animals forever!

Congratulations!

You are now officially
ANIMAL CRACKERS!

Hoppy's Animal Jokes

Q: What happens to a frog's car
when it breaks down?
A: It gets toad away.

Q: Why are frogs always so happy?
A: They eat whatever bugs them

Q: What type of sandals do frogs wear?
A: Open-toad!

Q: What do you call a girl with
a frog on her head?
A: Lily.

Q: Why couldn't the leopard play
hide and seek?
A: Because he was always spotted.

Q: How do you count cows?
A: With a cowculator.

Q: What do you call a fish without an eye?
A: Fsh!

Q: What goes tick-tock, bow-wow,
tick-tock, bow-wow?
A: A watch dog.

Q: What is the quietest kind of a dog?
A: A hush puppy.

Q: What do cats eat for breakfast?
A: Mice Krispies.

Q: What animal should you
never play cards with?
A: A cheetah.

Q: What is a cheetah's favourite food?
A: Fast food!

Q: Why did the snake cross the road?
A: To get to the other sssssside!

Q: What is the snake's
favourite subject?
A: Hiss-story

Q: Why did the dinosaur cross
the road?
A: Chickens didn't exist yet.

It's the way
I tell 'em!